Confronting Today's Issues

Confronting Today's Issues

Opportunities and Challenges for School Administrators

Chad Prosser, Denise Spirou,
and Jeffrey L. Buller

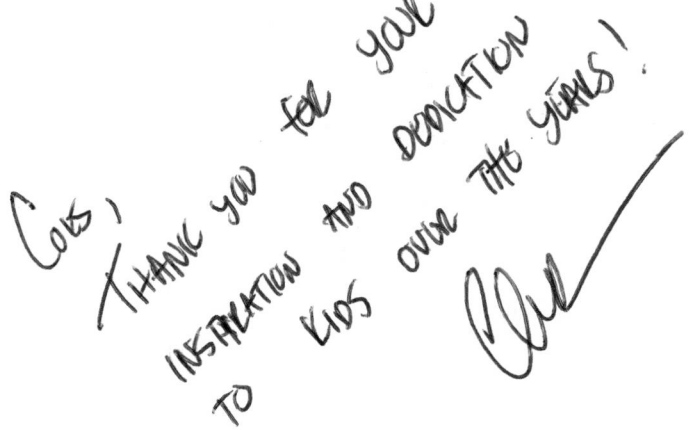

Cois,
Thank you for your
inspiration and dedication
to kids over the years!

ROWMAN & LITTLEFIELD
Lanham • Boulder • New York • London

Published by Rowman & Littlefield
An imprint of The Rowman & Littlefield Publishing Group, Inc.
4501 Forbes Boulevard, Suite 200, Lanham, Maryland 20706
https://rowman.com

6 Tinworth Street, London SE11 5AL, United Kingdom

British Library Cataloguing in Publication Information Available

Library of Congress Control Number: 2019952710
ISBN 978-1-4758-5045-1 (cloth : alk. paper)
ISBN 978-1-4758-5046-8 (pbk. : alk. paper)
ISBN 978-1-4758-5047-5 (electronic)

∞ ™ The paper used in this publication meets the minimum requirements of American National Standard for Information Sciences Permanence of Paper for Printed Library Materials, ANSI/NISO Z39.48-1992.

To Janet Burke, Michael J. Romano, Faith Waters, Ken LeCain, and Cynthia Tyson, and to the memory of Robert Vacca, the teachers and leaders who showed us the way.

Contents

Preface

School leadership is currently in a time of transition. That statement alone shouldn't surprise anyone. School leadership is *always* in a time of transition. Different generations of students have different needs. New challenges and opportunities constantly arise in society. Laws change. Parental expectations of schools evolve. *Societal* expectations of schools evolve. And administrators are at the forefront of both leading and responding to these larger changes.

Nevertheless, the current moment appears to be a singularly critical point in the history of education and of the role that teachers and administrators can play in creating the sort of schools that today's students deserve. As a result, academic leaders are eagerly seeking solutions to problems they haven't encountered before and ways of capitalizing on opportunities that have only recently arisen. This book provides the resources that these school leaders need to succeed in today's educational environment and to build the robust programs that their students deserve.

There certainly is no lack of existing resources for school administrators. Most of these resources contain excellent advice, and the best of that advice will be presented in the pages that follow, but too much of the literature created for teachers and administrators today is theoretical rather than practical and written in a cumbersome style that may be suited for a graduate course in education but that obscures rather than elucidates the advice it contains.

Confronting Today's Issues was written with two aims. First, it seeks to present field-tested solutions that work, not just in one school or system, but in a wide variety of educational environments, each with its own unique opportunities and challenges. Second, its style is intended to be accessible to anyone who hopes to maintain a superb educational program or improve a struggling one. It is devoid of jargon, presenting ideas clearly and avoiding the all-too-common tendency to veil relatively straightforward concepts behind technical vocabulary that none of us would tolerate from our own students.

The team assembled for this project brings together the skills and experience needed for the ambitious goals intended for this brief guide. The authors all have direct experience in education at a variety of levels and know firsthand what works and what doesn't in schools today.

- Chad Prosser has over fifteen years of experience in public education, where he has specialized in the creation of school improvement plans, safety and security, scheduling, stakeholder involvement, behavior management, and teacher evaluation and coaching.
- Denise Spirou is a highly effective leader who trains instructors, consults with principals, and provides superior leadership to teachers, support and guidance to parents, and educational direction to students.
- Jeffrey L. Buller is an experienced administrator in higher education whose numerous books, consultancies, and workshops are in demand all over the world.

We would also like to acknowledge Rebecca Peter, who provided valuable editorial assistance throughout this project, as well as our very supportive editors at Rowman & Littlefield, Tom Koerner and Carlie Wall.

As with any collaborative work, the opinions of one coauthor don't always precisely overlap those of the other coauthors. There may be observations in this book, therefore, that all three authors find intriguing, but don't entirely agree with. They hope you'll find these observations intriguing, too, even if you don't agree with all of them either.

In short, it is the authors' hope that, through this book, you'll gain insights on how to build on your own leadership strengths and make the types of choices that will improve your programs and your school. There is probably no other topic as important today as making sure that we're devoting our resources and creativity to innovative approaches that will help our students learn regardless of their socioeconomic background or challenges outside of school. While school administrators today do have an almost overwhelming number of challenges, they also have limitless opportunities, and it is the authors' goal to help you tap into those opportunities in the most effective way possible.

Introduction

Many of the opportunities and challenges facing today's schools are inseparable from one another. We can't help students overcome their academic obstacles if they're not learning in a safe and secure environment. We can have the best possible system in place for faculty and staff evaluation, but those processes are likely to be ineffective if we didn't hire the right people to begin with. And we can't create the schools that our students deserve if we don't budget our resources effectively and prove to be good stewards of the funds allocated to us.

For this reason, *Confronting Today's Issues* has been structured in such a way that each issue builds on the last. While it may be tempting to jump immediately to a topic of particular interest to you, we recommend that the chapters be read sequentially so that concepts introduced in early chapters can help inform and guide the discussions that appear in later chapters. Moreover, we recommend that readers review the list of key points that are included at the end of each chapter as a way of making sure they have mastered each set of recommendations and their rationale before moving on.

As a guide to contemporary issues in education, *Confronting Today's Issues* can be used in a number of ways:

- If you're an academic leader who wants to help the people in your school or system work together more effectively to make their programs better, this book will provide the ideas and examples you'll need in order to help others address the realities of education today more effectively. You can also mine it for ideas on how to build on your own strengths as a teacher or administrator and to improve in those areas where you may find challenges.

- If you're involved in a faculty and staff development program—or if you'd like to start one—this book can serve as a framework for the discussions and training sessions you conduct. Your participants will emerge from your program with not only a wealth of new ideas but also practical strategies that they can start putting in place immediately.
- If you're a professor in a college program on educational leadership, *Confronting Today's Issues* is appropriate as a textbook, providing the teachers and administrators of tomorrow with a toolkit of techniques that will be of lasting value to them throughout their own careers.
- If you're a student teacher or just starting out in the profession and want to gain insight into the challenges that school administrators need to deal with on a daily basis, this book can provide you with the insights you need in order to understand why certain decisions are made and how they might be made more effectively in the future.
- If you're a seasoned teacher who aspires to take on an administrative role, this book can serve as the blueprint for your leadership vision while also giving you background in the steps you'll need to take in order to make that vision a reality.

At the end of each chapter, you'll find a carefully selected set of resources that can assist you in taking the ideas of this book further. The materials under the reference section are mentioned in the text itself; the resources section provides additional material that goes beyond what we've been able to include in that chapter. In either case, if you wish to continue exploring the issue of building an outstanding academic program, these are the materials that we most highly recommend.

The improvement of schools is a process and not a destination. We will never reach a point where we have perfected every aspect of how schools are designed, staffed, and organized, and the approaches that work in one locale may not be as effective in another. Nevertheless, developing robust and outstanding schools is as exciting a journey as we can imagine, and we're pleased that you've decided to join us on it.

Chapter One

A New Model of School Leadership

As the world has changed significantly in the last twenty years, so have the needs of the learner. No longer are schools expected to teach students simply to memorize facts and comply with directives; the twenty-first-century learner is expected to be creative and a critical thinker.

With this shift in the requirements for students and, in turn, the role of the school, the primary responsibilities of the school leader are considerably different from what was expected in the past. The days of the school leader spending the majority of his or her time handling minor disciplinary issues have been replaced by the expectation that the school leader—who often has a title like *principal* or *head of school*—is the "lead learner" in a team of committed co-learners. School leaders are entrusted with creating a culture within their school in which teaching and learning occur at high levels.

With the era of high-stakes testing, school leaders are continually forced to look for new ways to improve performance at their schools. Increased demands for accountability from accrediting agencies, legislatures, local governments, parents, and other groups have led to an expectation that school leaders can analyze data effectively and use that data to make informed decisions.

Fortunately, the increased use of technology in schools has made the collection of data easier than ever. In addition to the wealth of information leaders can obtain about student learning from classroom management software, standardized tests, and computer-assisted instruction, it's now possible for administrators to know virtually everything that happens in their schools because of the connected technological systems known as the internet of things (IoT).

Some of those connected systems include smart lighting and HVAC, facial recognition technology, wireless door locks and temperature monitors, interactive whiteboards, IP surveillance cameras and other sensor-equipped items. Schools are even using IoT technology to *monitor and track school buses* and student attendance. (Andrade 2018)

But school leaders can't depend on technology alone. Effective data-informed decision-making requires input from many sources, and school leaders are charged by superintendents and others to make sure that they have buy-in from all their stakeholders in order to achieve the highest level of improvement. For this reason most of all, *effective school leaders create a culture in which school improvement initiatives are teacher led.*

Nevertheless, today's school leaders cannot rely on data alone either. They must also be able to create a plan that will guide their school improvement process. As the Education Improvement Commission notes in its handbook for administrators, "[a] school improvement plan is a road map that sets out the changes a school needs to make to improve the level of student achievement, and shows how and when these changes will be made" (Education Improvement Commission 2000, p. 6). And, as anyone who has ever initiated a change process knows, change is hard and likely to be met with resistance at many levels.

So, doing what is necessary to change processes at a school in such a way that everyone is working together to improve student learning can initially seem to be an arduous task. But the best approach to the challenges school leaders face today can be summarized by a single theme that the authors have repeatedly found to be effective in their own work and to which they will refer repeatedly in the chapters that follow: *start by paying attention to culture and mission.*

If you don't begin with this basic principle, all the strategies, techniques, and best practices that you learn about in your coursework, witness at other schools, or read about in books are likely to be ineffective in the long run. Teachers, members of the staff and administration, and even the students need to know the following:

- Who are we as a school?
- What are our core values?
- What are our most important goals?
- Why are those goals meaningful?
- Where do we collectively see ourselves going from here?

All too often, meetings and in-service training focus on the problem of the day. The result is that members of the school lose track of the big picture. Administrators resort to what might be called whack-a-mole leadership:

when a problem arises, they "whack" it, only to move on then to the next problem and then the next. The spirit that this approach conveys is that a school exists largely as a series of problems to be solved, rather than as a community that can enable each member (faculty and staff as well as students) to grow as individuals and reach their true potential.

Teachers and administrators sometimes complain that students don't easily make connections between concepts in the same discipline or between their various disciplines. They don't apply the mathematical skills that they have learned to their chemistry courses, the insights into culture they have gained in their social studies courses to their understanding of literature, or the lessons they have learned in English classes about effective writing to the essays they create for other subjects.

But how are students supposed to be able to see the connections when the schools themselves function as merely a group of disconnected units, disconnected problems to be solved, and disconnected people who merely happen to teach and learn in the same place?

The very first step, therefore, in confronting today's challenges for schools is to help create an environment where every member of the community knows and cares about mission and values. Instead of the *reactive* approach of trying to solve whatever problem comes across their desk that day, school leaders need to become more *proactive* in discussing shared values and goals.

Problem solving can be divisive. Everyone has his or her own favorite solution to the problem and may resent the fact that others prefer different approaches, but discussing culture and mission is unifying. It reminds people of what they share instead of what isolates them from others. It is the prerequisite to absolutely everything else that effective school leaders achieve.

APPRECIATIVE INQUIRY

One approach that school leaders can take as a way of not only discussing culture and mission but also creating the model that will move schools forward is the practice known as *appreciative inquiry*.

In most school improvement plans, the strategy that administrators are following is to identify what isn't working, find the cause of what isn't working, and repair what isn't working. That's an effective technique when it comes to fixing the HVAC system or improving the efficiency of school bus routes, but it isn't the most effective strategy when it comes to working with people.

The message that people often hear when a school leader asks, "What isn't working here?" is "I see my role as figuring out *who* the problem is here." And once members of the faculty and staff start believing that administrators see them as problems instead of solutions, the result is once again divisive instead of unifying.

Even worse, when school leaders try to institute improvements by finding problems to solve, they soon begin to see problems everywhere. They convey the impression that their job is to catch people doing what's wrong rather than support them in doing what's right.

A concept that is commonly taught in teacher preparation programs is Robert Rosenthal and Lenore Jacobson's theory of the Pygmalion Effect: students tend to perform up to the expectations teachers have of them, and so it is more effective to expect greatness than mediocrity (Rosenthal and Jacobson 1968). The negative corollary of Rosenthal and Jacobson's theory is sometimes known as the Golem Effect: Students tend to perform down to the low expectations teachers have of them.

What is sometimes less apparent is that members of the faculty and staff are also influenced by the Pygmalion and Golem Effects: they tend to perform up or down to the expectations school leaders have of them (as demonstrated in Bezuijen, van den Berg, van Dam, and Thierry 2009). So, if a school leader conveys (even unintentionally) that people are problems, they begin to see themselves as problems and, all too frequently, they *become* problems. A far more effective approach to school improvement is to ask, "What's working here, and how can we do more of it? How can we build on those strengths we already have?"

Appreciative inquiry thus begins by identifying those times when the school was at its best. What had just occurred? What made members of the faculty and staff proud to work there? What made students proud to attend there? What can we learn from our moments of greatest success? As the positive psychology advocate Michelle McQuaid notes, "Appreciative Inquiry uses a simple 4D cycle to guide these questions—discover, dream, design, deploy—and create changes that last." For example by:

- *Discovering* stories of what happens when you feel most alive, engaged and proud of your work helps create the confidence and momentum that unleashes higher levels of performance. You might ask, "When you feel engaged, energized and enjoying life, what's happening?"
- *Dreaming* vivid positive images of your future can pull you forward with optimism and hope and motivate you to take positive action. You might ask, "If you could do what you've just described more consistently, what might be possible as you look ahead?"
- *Design* invites you to create multiple pathways to turn your dreams into reality by identifying and prioritizing ways to move from where you are right now to where you want to be. You might ask, "How can you move from where you are right now, to where you want to be?"

- *Deploy* invites people to volunteer to take responsibility for the changes they feel passionate enough to put into action. You might ask, "If there was one action you could take, where would you be willing to start?" (McQuade 2018).

It's easy to understand why approaching school improvement in this way is a lot more likely to engage the most creative energies of the faculty and staff than by asking questions that sound to them (despite how they sound to you) like, "What's wrong with you people?"

In practical terms, appreciative inquiry can be incorporated into a new model of school leadership by encouraging members of the faculty and staff to identify the school's particular strengths and points of pride. This brainstorming activity can be completed in person, during a teacher training day, or online by using a listserv or threaded discussion.

Then, when this process is complete, the complete list should be reviewed, and, with all participants actively engaged, the following observations should be removed:

- Our faculty and staff are excellent (or superb, accomplished, distinguished, dedicated, engaged, passionate, or similar terms of praise).
- We are committed to excellence.
- We care about our students.
- We're student-oriented.
- We value professionalism. (Or, "We are professionals.")
- We accomplish a great deal even though our funding is inadequate. (Or, "We do a lot with a little.")

The reason why these observations will not be useful in the next stage of the process is that they're overly generic. *Every* school believes that its faculty and staff are excellent, care about students, value professionalism, and so on. Even if you yourself might feel that another school is failing in these areas, the people who work there believe these truths about themselves. In other words, the bullet points listed above don't indicate what makes a school *distinctive*; they indicate what a school *is*.

The most important requirement for your list of strengths or points of pride is that it should contain only those elements that most people, even those who don't work at the school, would regard as its distinctive assets. If at all possible, have members of the school community keep paring the list down until it consists of no more than five or six truly distinguishing traits.

Then, as a way of reinforcing the culture and mission of the school, have that list posted in every classroom, hallway, and stairwell on campus. Since those strengths are part of your school's unique DNA, everyone who is part of the school community should be made to *feel* that they are part of what makes them special, that they are part of their identity.

ARISTOTLE AND THE FIVE WHYS

The next step in building your new model of school leadership is to build on these strengths in such a way that excellence becomes, not a goal that people strive for, but standard operating procedure for everyone who works and studies in your community. You achieve this goal by engaging in *root cause analysis* to determine what it is that helped develop these strengths in the first place. Ordinarily when school leaders engage in root cause analysis, they're trying to determine why certain problems exist. Why does the school suffer from so much vandalism? Why are reading scores lagging behind the state average? Why are attendance rates declining?

Proceeding in that way, however, will not help you create the sort of school your students deserve. As we saw before, when you start looking for problems, soon all you see are problems. On the other hand, when you start exploring the causes of strengths, soon much of what you see consists of new possibilities.

A basic technique used in identifying the sources of strengths is nearly as old as schools are themselves. For example, the ancient Athenian philosopher Aristotle (384–322 BCE) believed that everything people do is done for a reason. In other words, if you saw someone doing something and asked the person why he or she was doing it, only someone who was utterly lacking in self-reflection would be unable to provide you with an answer. But you could also keep this line of questioning going since nearly every motive people had was inspired in turn by another underlying motive.

Imagine that you're walking through a suburban neighborhood one day, and you happen to see one of your students mowing the lawn at a residence that you happen to know is not where that student lives. "Why are you mowing the grass here?" you might ask.

Student: I'm just trying to make a little extra money.

You: Why do you want extra money?

Student: Because there's a concert I want to go to with my friends.

You: Why do you want to go to that concert?

Student: Because my friends and I always have fun when we go out.

You: Why do you want to have fun?

Student: I don't know. I guess having fun just makes me happy.

And there, Aristotle says, that whole line of questioning has to come to a dead end. It makes no sense to ask anyone, "Why do you want to be happy?" because happiness is always a good in and of itself. Every line of reasoning we ever ask about someone's motivation has to end there. Ultimately, people do everything they do out of a desire to be happy.

When, therefore, you're engaging in root cause analysis, the end of any chain of investigation will always be an observation like, "We're doing [WHATEVER WE'RE DOING] in order to be happy." But if our goal is to improve our schools and develop an effective model of school leadership, we don't need to take our series of questions all the way to the end. You already know that people's final motivation will be the pursuit of happiness, so we can learn a great deal about shared goals, values, and motivations by examining how people describe their incentives *a few steps before the end* of Aristotle's series of questions.

The general rule of thumb in root cause analysis is that you can discover what you need to know in order to improve a process by carrying your series of explorations down about five levels. This process is known as the Five Whys. Many discussions of the Five Whys relate this approach to problem solving. They start with an observation like "There's too much graffiti outside the cafeteria" and seek to understand the underlying reasons for that problem. The result is something like the following:

There's too much graffiti outside the cafeteria.

Why? Vandals know they're unlikely to be caught there.

Why? There is no fence preventing access to the rear cafeteria area from 89th Street, no exterior lighting on that side of the building, and no twenty-four-hour security for the building.

Why? Neither the maintenance and improvement budget nor the staff personnel budget are large enough for these expenditures.

Why? State funding for schools was cut again this year.

Why? The party controlling the state legislature has priorities that do not include adequate school funding.

As in this example, when the Five Whys are used for problem solving, the result often becomes little more than the assignment of blame, a "solution" that doesn't really address the problem, or both. In our hypothetical example, it may feel momentarily satisfying to blame the state legislature for its short-sightedness, but it doesn't bring you any closer to eliminating the graffiti.

The Five Whys can really become powerful in building a new model of school leadership to redirect the culture and mission of a school when this process is combined with appreciative inquiry. In other words, rather than beginning your exploration with the identification of a problem, begin with the identification of a strength or point of pride such as in the following example:

Morale at Mamie Eisenhower Middle School is always at its highest on the first day of school.

Why? People come to the school in a good mood, and that mood carries over to their teaching and learning.

Why? The frustrations and disappointments of the previous year seem remote and unimportant.

Why? Faculty, staff, and students all feel rested, and there is a sense that anything is possible.

Why? A new school year offers new beginnings, and people recoup their energy over the break.

Why? New beginnings mean that, if last year was good, this year can be even better; if last year was bad, this year can be different. And people have the energy to begin working on those goals.

If you were the principal or head of school at Mamie Eisenhower Middle School, this series of questions now might give you an idea of what you can do to make the school even better: You need to increase the opportunities people have to feel that new beginnings where anything is possible occur more frequently than once a year and to seek strategies where exhaustion and apathy are least likely to derail those goals.

Depending on your specific situation and what is possible locally, your efforts might range anywhere from merely adopting a new school motto ("Mamie Eisenhower Middle School: Where New Beginnings Happen Every Day") to implementing a radical new year-round school calendar where each six weeks of time in school is followed by a two-week break when faculty, staff, and students will all have time to recharge and renew.

No matter what plan you have moving forward, it is likely to be far more practical and productive than merely wringing your hands about continued budget cuts and blaming politicians whose minds you have few, if any, opportunities to change.

SETTING SMART GOALS AND THEN MAKING THEM SMARTER

One of the problems school leaders frequently encounter when trying to develop a positive mission and culture is creating a set of goals that initially seem appropriate but that don't provide the sort of guidance that members of the school community actually need. They make it their objective to do things like improve morale, enhance security, and promote better ties to the community. But how can you tell when you've actually accomplished what you set out to do? How will you determine whether morale has indeed improved, people are more secure, and ties with the community have been developed to the degree you would like?

In 1981, George Doran, Arthur Miller, and James Cunningham proposed a simple acronym that is useful in phrasing goals so that not only will they more likely be accomplished but also people can demonstrate to others that these goals have been accomplished. Their mnemonic device was to make sure that the goals you set are SMART, with the letters in SMART standing for Specific, Measurable, Achievable, Responsible, and Time-Related (Doran, Miller, and Cunningham 1981).

Since Doran, Miller, and Cunningham (1981) published their original article in *Management Review*, many other authors have attempted to improve their original acronym.

> Achievable is sometimes replaced with Attainable, Appropriate, or Ambitious; Responsible is sometimes exchanged for Relevant, Reasonable, or Results-Based; and Time-Related is sometimes rephrased as Timely, Time-Specific, or something similar. (Buller 2018, p. 55)

But there is one important problem with SMART Goals that none of these variations was able to address.

> The specificity of SMART goals is a great cure for the worst sins of goal setting—ambiguity and irrelevance ("We are going to delight our customers every day in every way!"). But SMART goals are better for steady-state situations than for change situations, because the assumptions underlying them are that the goals are worthwhile. . . . SMART goals presume the emotion; they don't generate it. . . . There are some people whose hearts are set aflutter by goals such as "improving the liquidity ratio by 30 percent over the next 18 months." They're called accountants. (Heath and Heath 2013, p. 82)

In other words, by the time you burrow down to the level of specificity required by the SMART Goals formula, goals simply aren't very exciting. Teachers and staff members work in schools because they have a passion for improving the lives of students, not because they want to "reduce the level of absenteeism by half over the course of seventeen weeks."

The problem with SMART Goals is that they're suited more to the mindset people adopt with *problem-solving approaches* than that associated with *appreciative inquiry*. But that problem can be solved if you simply make your SMART Goals SMARTER. That is to say, add two essential elements missing from the original formulation proposed by Doran, Miller, and Cunningham: enthusiasm and rewards.

Enthusiasm consists of reflecting on what people get excited about and actually care about at your school. Since no one takes a job as a member of the faculty or staff because they expect to become wealthy, what attracted them to this line of work in the first place? Think of what the vast majority of school employees are like when they're initially hired. They're driven, committed, and energetic in their desire to make a positive difference. Many of our employees never lose that level of commitment, but some do. What sort of goals might restore them to the engagement and passion they once had?

Rewards involve identifying how members of a community recognize progress as benefiting themselves. There can be momentary pleasure in checking off an objective on a to-do list, but many people long for something more, some greater sense that what they do *matters*. If you set a goal of identifying ways in which members of the faculty and staff can improve reading scores by 8 percent over two years, you'll have a goal that everyone at the school can work toward, but will they be excited about it?

On the other hand, if you explain that goal in terms of how members of the school community will change students' lives by causing more of them to remain enrolled and graduate, teachers and staff members are likely to feel that the extra effort required to reach the goal isn't a sacrifice; it's a privilege. They will feel rewarded just by accomplishing a meaningful task.

What all of this means is that, as a school leader, you'll need to become bilingual. But you don't need to become bilingual in the sense of developing fluency in another language (although that's an admirable skill for school leaders to develop) but in the sense of how you explain your goals to others. When interacting with superintendents, system representatives, and accrediting bodies, focus on the first five letters in SMARTER Goals.

When speaking to the faculty and staff, emphasize the last two. You're not changing the message, merely speaking of the message in "language" that resonates with that particular audience. Superintendents, system representatives, and accrediting bodies care about quantifiable, objective goals. Members of the faculty and staff care about goals that relate to a larger, socially constructive purpose. SMARTER Goals address both of these concerns, but not all of your stakeholders care about all seven parts of that acronym. (For more on how to make SMART Goals SMARTER, see Buller 2018, pp. 55–60.)

WHEN YOU *NEED* TO SOLVE PROBLEMS

One reservation that school leaders sometimes have about appreciative inquiry and the emphasis on culture and mission recommended in this book is their fear that this approach may not help them deal with the genuine and severe problems facing their school. "I can talk all I want about making the world a better place and creating the type of school our students deserve," they might say, "but the reality in which I work is one of gang violence, substance abuse, children whose only meal of the day is the hot lunch we provide, and a physical plant that was outdated twenty years ago. I don't have the luxury of all this 'think positive' advice."

The authors in no way want to ignore the fact that schools facing serious, heartbreaking problems do exist in large numbers and that there are occasions when these problems simply cannot be ignored. At the same time, it's important to recognize that even severe problems are rarely solved simply by fixating on the problems. There are situations in which appreciative inquiry and a focus on culture and mission do need to be complemented (not replaced) by some creative problem solving. But there are also right ways and wrong ways of doing so.

The wrong way to solve problems is to leap immediately to implementing a solution without determining whether it will actually solve the given problem, begin imposing organization-wide remedies that do not have the support and commitment of those who will have to sustain them, and fail to consider possible side effects of the proposed solution. The right way to solve problems is to develop team-based approaches that are high impact and high leverage.

A *high-impact solution* is one that goes far beyond surface symptoms to address the root cause of a problem. A *high-leverage solution* is one in which the results far outweigh the investment of time, effort, and resources. High-impact and high-leverage solutions have three distinct characteristics:

- *They have one-time rather than continuing costs.* It's better to eliminate a severe bacterial infection with a single course of antibiotics than to keep treating the symptoms with pain relievers. In much the same way, it's better to address the pilfering of supplies by installing a new type of lock than by posting a twenty-four-hour guard over the supply cabinet. High-impact, high-leverage solutions generally fall under the rubric of "working smarter, not harder." They may involve initial costs or require intense short-term effort, but they shouldn't involve ongoing expenditures of resources better used elsewhere.
- *They should require minimal and unavoidable risks.* Any initiative brings with it the possibility of unintended consequences. Those consequences can be reduced by thinking carefully about what could possibly go wrong (because all too often it will). Schools are complex organizations with many interconnected parts. For this reason, leaders carefully study the system to see where connections exist or may exist before making any changes to the system. They prepare backup plans and exit strategies in case something goes wrong. Where possible, they test possible solutions in small groups before implementing them school-wide. And they create contingency plans for as many possibilities as they can foresee.
- *They should produce other benefits besides just solving the problem.* Imagine that a school has high maintenance costs due to the wear and tear on

facilities that are caused simply by students moving from one classroom to another. Revising the schedule so that students do not have to transition as far from one course to another (or, even more radically, having certain teachers change classrooms while the students remain in place) may address that problem while also producing other benefits: fewer student injuries, more efficient use of the school day, less absenteeism caused by students who simply leave the building instead of going to their next class, and so on.

A CASE STUDY IN SCHOOL LEADERSHIP

Much of what administrators learn about leadership is developed through experience, not theoretical analysis. Your own experience will prove to be your best guide to the leadership approaches that work best for you. Nevertheless, as a way of accelerating the learning process, the authors have developed a case study based on the material of each chapter.

Although each case study is followed by a set of suggestions about how best to handle the issues raised by the case, don't immediately proceed to that section after reading the scenario. Instead, formulate your own ideas about how best to proceed and then compare your ideas to the suggestions the authors provide. Here is your first case.

Evan Elpus was recently hired to serve as the principal of Not So Great Expectations Elementary School. Evan was recruited to be a change agent, and certainly change was needed. The school regularly scored at the bottom of its district in standardized test scores, had a very high turnover rate for teachers, led the state in student absenteeism, and had a physical plant that was badly out of date. Evan knew that his challenges would be great when his friends began sending him sympathy cards as soon as he accepted the job.

Evan decided that the best way to bring about a cultural change quickly was to begin addressing the school's problems in one-on-one sessions with each member of the faculty and staff. He would begin these sessions by saying something like, "I need you to help me understand how Not So Great Expectations Elementary School got into its current predicament. What are people doing wrong, and what do I need to do to fix it?"

He would then share a story or two about his successes at his previous school, Deeply Endowed Private Academy, as a way of encouraging the faculty and staff that success was indeed possible.

When Evan had collected all the information he could from these private conversation, he prepared a detailed PowerPoint presentation listing each of the school's failings (in priority order), the probable root cause of that problem, and three or four changes each person could make in order to begin addressing that deficiency. "I know the challenge seems great, but I can help you do better than you've done. Why, only two or three years ago at Deeply Endowed Private Academy, we faced a similar challenge when our Asian Language Immersion Lab was getting to be out of date."

He then went on to describe how the school's successful capital campaign was able to address this problem as well as several others.

How successful do you believe Evan will be as principal of Not So Great Expectations Elementary School? How might you have handled the situation differently?

DISCUSSION OF THE CASE STUDY

As was mentioned earlier, be sure that you have decided your own thoughts about this case before continuing to read the following recommendations. The purpose of a case study isn't to give you the one "right" answer; it's to provide you with practice in thinking through complex situations before you have to deal with leadership challenges at your own school. After all, the cases presented in this book aren't likely to occur exactly as written during your own career. But thinking through these issues can help to refine your own leadership skills and decision-making process.

In addition, your own circumstances may mean that the best answer for you isn't necessarily the best answer for someone else. So, the recommendations provided by the authors are based on their own training and experience as academic leaders. They can't be aware of all the conditions that might make their suggestions less than appropriate in your particular situation. If, therefore, you've already developed your thoughts about the case of Evan Elpus and Not So Great Expectations Elementary School, compare your ideas with those below.

Evan seems to have fallen into the familiar trap of trying to bring about substantive change at his school by jumping immediately to problem solving rather than trying to identify what's working well at the school. His one-on-one conversations with members of the faculty and staff are likely to be perceived by them as efforts to determine who's at fault for the school's poor performance. His style will create an us-versus-them division between the administration and others.

For example, much of what Evan says conveys the idea, "You've created this problem, and I'm here to save you." That division is intensified by his habit of contrasting his current school (unfavorably) with his former school, an institution that seems to have been in a very different financial situation from Not So Great Expectations Elementary School.

If you were confronted by Evan's challenges, it probably would have been far preferable to begin by determining what the school is doing right rather than what it is doing wrong. Even if the successes you find are very few, they can form the nucleus of a team spirit that will begin to make further successes possible.

By beginning your term at the school with appreciative inquiry and a focus on mission, culture, and values, you're much more likely to bring about positive change than you are if you start looking only for problems. As an outsider, you'll need to create an atmosphere of trust and shared responsibility before you can expect to see genuine improvement.

KEY POINTS IN THIS CHAPTER

- Since schools have changed significantly over the past twenty years, the role of the principal or head of school must also change. School administrators must see their roles as "lead learners" in a team of committed co-learners.
- Effective school leaders create a culture in which school improvement initiatives are teacher led.
- Appreciative inquiry is a more effective means of improving the mission and culture of a school than the identification of problems and the assignment of blame.
- Students live up or down to the expectations we have of them. So do members of the faculty and staff.
- Combined with appreciative inquiry, the process known as the Five Whys can be a powerful tool in building a new model of school leadership.
- Making SMART Goals SMARTER helps ensure that objectives are not only well-defined but also inspiring.
- When school leaders do need to engage in problem solving, they should seek high-impact and high-leverage solutions.

REFERENCES

Andrade, D. 2018. "How the Internet of Things May Change K–12 Culture." *EdTech*, December 5, 2018. https://edtechmagazine.com/k12/k12/k12/higher/article/2018/12/how-internet-things-may-change-k-12-culture

Bezuijen, X., P. van den Berg, K. van Dam., & H. Thierry. 2009. "Pygmalion and Employee Learning: The Role of Leader Behaviors." *Journal of Management* 35(5): 1248–267.

Buller, J. L. 2018. *Managing Time and Stress: A Guide for Academic Leaders to Accomplish What Matters.* Lanham, MD: Rowman & Littlefield.

Doran, G., A. Miller, & C. Cunningham. 1981. "There's a S.M.A.R.T. Way to Write Management's Goals and Objectives." *Management Review* 70(11): 35–36.

Education Improvement Commission. 2000. *School Improvement Planning: A Handbook.* http://www.edu.gov.on.ca/eng/document/reports/sihande.pdf

Heath, C., & D. Heath. 2013. *Switch: How to Change Things When Change Is Hard.* New York, NY: Random House.

McQuade, M. 2018. "Are You Asking the Right Questions?" https://www.michellemcquaid.com/asking-right-questions/

Rosenthal, R., & L. Jacobson. 1968. *Pygmalion in the Classroom: Teacher Expectation and Pupils' Intellectual Development.* New York, NY: Holt, Rinehart and Winston.

RESOURCES

Bambrick-Santoyo, P. 2018. *Leverage Leadership 2.0: A Practical Guide to Building Exceptional Schools* (2nd ed.). San Francisco, CA: Jossey-Bass.

Eckert, J. 2018. *Leading Together: Teachers and Administrators Improving Student Outcomes.* Thousand Oaks. CA: Corwin.

Gorton, R. A., & J. A. Alston. 2019. *School Leadership & Administration: Important Concepts, Case Studies, & Simulations* (10th ed.). New York, NY: McGraw-Hill Education.

Hebert, E. A. 2006. *"The Boss of the Whole School": Effective Leadership in Action.* New York, NY: Teachers College Press.

Johnson, J., S. Leibowitz, & K. Perret. 2017. *The Coach Approach to School Leadership: Leading Teachers to Higher Levels of Effectiveness.* Alexandria, VA: ASCD.

Jones, I. C., V. Blake, & W. R. Daggett. 2018. *Fearless Conversations School Leaders Have to Have.* Thousand Oaks, CA: Corwin.

Klimek, K. J., E. Ritzenhein, & K. D. Sullivan. 2008. *Generative Leadership: Shaping New Futures for Today's Schools.* Thousand Oaks, CA: Corwin.

Lewis, R. E., & P. Winkelman. 2017. *Lifescaping Practices in School Communities: Implementing Action Research and Appreciative Inquiry.* New York, NY: Routledge.

Chapter Two

The Elephant in Every Room

Safe Schools and Security

The issue of school safety immediately confronts every administrator with a paradox. On the one hand, there is strong evidence that the safest possible place for children, particularly in their earliest years, is in school (Goldstein 2018; Hiltzik 2018; Toppo 2013). On the other hand, there were more recorded cases of school shootings in the first eighteen years of the twenty-first century than there were in the entire twentieth century (Katsiyannis, Whitford, and Ennis 2018).

Because of the attention given to such issues as bullying and school violence, teachers and administrators have made their schools far safer than they were in the 1980s and 1990s (Fox and Fridel 2018). But those schools are often *perceived* by parents (and sometimes by students themselves) to be far less safe (Perumean-Chaney and Sutton 2013).

How can a school leader deal effectively with such contradictory information? How can they achieve all the other goals needed to create the type of schools that today's students deserve when they know that school safety and security is the elephant in the room during every conversation with a parent, board member, or legislator?

The answer to these questions is that the duty of a school leader when it comes to safe schools and security is always twofold: to make sure the students and stakeholders of the school *are* safe and to make sure the students and stakeholders of the school *feel* safe. There's a great deal of difference between being prepared and creating an environment of fear. The mistake that some schools make is to err on one side or the other of these two alternatives. Let's explore some best practices of how to achieve a more balanced approach.

IDENTIFYING POTENTIAL DANGERS

It's important to make one point absolutely clear from the beginning: It will never be possible to predict and thus prevent every danger that can threaten schools and their students.

Before the shooting at Colorado's Columbine High School in 1999, very few teachers and administrators regarded mass shootings as a potential threat. Now, however, it would be the height of irresponsibility for school administrators not to take the possibility of active-shooter scenarios into account during their strategies for safety preparedness. In a similar way, natural disasters are not always predictable, but their possibility must be considered if every member of a school community is to work and learn in a safe environment.

The fundamental principle of effective safety and security, therefore, is to plan for what you can anticipate; prepare for what you can't. Among the potential dangers of which school leaders can and should be aware are the following:

- Fires
- The presence and use of guns on campus
- Bombs and bomb threats
- Death threats directed either generally or to specific individuals
- Abductions by parents or others
- Natural dangers (such as tornadoes, earthquakes, and hurricanes) that may reasonably be expected in the school's location
- Bullying, including cyberbullying
- Gang-related violence
- Fights and other types of physical violence or intimidation
- Social isolation and other causes of depression or anxiety
- Sexual exploitation
- Injury caused by school facilities or equipment
- Vehicular accidents either on campus or while students are on their way to or from school

Although it's impossible to predict the potential dangers that may arise in the future, *planning* to eliminate these known threats is an important first step in *preparing* to minimize unknown threats.

Useful resources, containing checklists and inventories, to help schools assess and identify potential dangers include Ortiz (2011); Fein, Vossekuil, Pollack, Borum, Modzeleski, and Reddy (2004); and Woods (n.d.). Those interested specifically in resources on how to assess written threats in terms of their severity and the potential for violence should consult Van Brunt (2016) and *Threat Assessment Template* (n.d.).

REDUCING OR ELIMINATING POTENTIAL DANGERS

While specific strategies are effective in reducing or eliminating these potential dangers, it's important to begin by reiterating a point that arose in chapter 1: start by paying attention to culture and mission. Providing physical protections is important, but those protections can only go so far. The single most important factor in creating a safe school environment is developing a culture in which safety is a core value and where members of the community view themselves as having the privilege of keeping one another safe.

Consider, for example, the Safety & Security Mission Statement of the Cherry Creek School District, less than an hour away from where the Columbine High School shooting occurred.

> The Cherry Creek School District is committed to creating safe, respectful, and inclusive learning environments where all community members work together to promote academic excellence, civil behaviors, and social competence. All staff, students, and parents help create safe schools. (Cherry Creek School District #5 n.d.)

This statement makes it clear that it is a shared value for members of the school community to look out for one another and keep each other safe. Safety is not the responsibility of security personnel alone; *everyone* in the school community plays a role.

In addition, this mission statement does not treat safety and security in isolation. It links these topics to academic excellence and behaving as part of a civil environment. When members of the community fail to live up to these high standards, an opportunity arises for *any* member of the community to remind their colleagues that such behavior doesn't reflect who they are and aspire to be. A commitment to safety is thus not just something that members of the staff must undertake. It is part of the school's DNA and an important element of its educational mission.

A code of conduct is important because it makes clear the types of behaviors that will not be tolerated. But a statement of values is also desirable because it makes clear the types of behaviors that are *expected*. A carefully considered statement of values thus plays a role in both safety and education: it helps build the type of community where people look out for one another, feel connected, develop empathy, and demonstrate respect for their peers. The result is greater security for the students and an important lesson in what positive civic behavior entails.

When all members of a school community take responsibility for one another's safety, they become proactive in identifying and eliminating potential dangers before disasters occur. They feel free to report when electrical cords are frayed, security doors are propped open, or one of their fellow community members appears to be in distress. Security cameras can be a wonderful resource for making schools safer, but they can't cover everywhere danger may be.

When each student, parent, teacher, administrator, and staff member understands that mutual protection and support are fundamental values of the community, everyone acts as a monitor for everyone else's safety and security, and people not only *are* safer; they also *feel* safer.

A focus on culture and mission does not, however, mean that routine security measures are unnecessary. Steps must still be taken to make sure that there are monitored and limited points of access to a school facility but multiple means of exit during an emergency.

Mandatory sign-in procedures with identity verification need to be in place for all visitors, who should then be issued identification badges that are valid only for the dates and times related to their visit. Doors and windows have to be tested to make certain that they are airtight in case environmental hazards arise.

Regular safety drills need to be conducted for multiple scenarios so that teachers and students know how to act almost as a reflex during times of emergency. Close relationships should be maintained with state and local law enforcement agencies so that they can provide expert guidance on additional measures that will help protect the community.

Those relationships will also ensure that the school's own emergency preparedness plan is appropriately aligned with the recommendations of the Department of Homeland Security, the Federal Emergency Management Agency, and other relevant national, state, and local authorities.

A candid assessment of the school's surrounding community can also help administrators prepare for potential situations that may be far more unlikely at other schools. For example, is there school located in an area where facilities commonly suffer from vandalism? Does the state or local registry indicate that there are known sex offenders in the area? Are there indications of local gang activity? Although no one can predict all the natural disasters that may affect any particular school, which weather- or geology-related dangers are most common in the region?

The school's individual mission may also have an impact on the types of measures that need to be taken in order to promote greater safety. For example, a school with a science or technology focus will probably have greater amounts of chemicals, specialized types of equipment, and far more hazardous materials on-site than humanities-based or comprehensive schools do. Schools with large intramural or district athletic programs will have sports facilities and equipment that will require regular maintenance and monitoring for potential problems.

When preparing students for how to act during various types of emergencies, the goal should be to conduct drills often enough to keep the students' emergency response skills fresh, but not so often to cause a climate of fear to permeate the school. A good rule of thumb is to conduct one emergency preparedness drill a month and to rotate among the different types of responses that may be necessary: evacuation (such as may be necessary during a fire), sheltering in place (such as may be necessary during a lockdown or earthquake), and moving to safer quarters (such as may be necessary during a flood, hurricane, or tornado).

Some schools have begun the practice of conducting highly realistic intruder drills in which one or more people, usually law enforcement officials, will enter the school carrying (unloaded) weapons and acting as though they are genuinely there to harm the students and faculty. That practice is rarely advisable. In a worst-case scenario, someone who isn't aware that a drill is taking place may actually harm or even kill those who are pretending to be intruders. Even in a best-case scenario, the experience can be so frightening to students that their anxiety and reluctance to attend school may increase. These highly realistic intruder drills can also lead to a "Boy Who Cried Wolf Syndrome" in which students become so used to drills that they fail to take an actual intrusion seriously.

A better approach is usually to engage in what is called a *soft lockdown*. In these scenarios, it is clearly announced that a drill is taking place. Appropriate doors are locked, and shelter is sought according to where students and teachers happen to be.

> During a Soft Lockdown the building perimeter is secured with staff stationed at the doors. Visitors may not enter the building during a "soft lockdown." Teaching proceeds as usual. Depending on the conditions, class period changes are allowed. Some schools have protocols with options to collect cell phones with the objective of preventing misinformation or confusion of communication with friends and family outside of the school. Some schools release part-time employees in a "soft lockdown" situation. (Soft Lockdown: Definition 2009.)

Local authorities may also have their own schedule for the types of drills that must be conducted and the frequency with which they must occur. These drills underscore the community's commitment to safety and the obligation each member has to ensure the health and welfare of every other member.

Conducting too many safety drills can, in the long run, be nearly as harmful to many students as conducting too few. A number of studies have suggested that repeating active-shooter drills causes its own type of posttraumatic stress in some children (Hamblin 2018; Rich and Cox 2018; Malafronte 2018). Determining the frequency of drills implying that someone may be out to harm the students has to take into account the need to protect students both physically and mentally. This situation is one where periodic practice is desirable but excessively repeated practice is likely to have serious unintended consequences.

Even though you don't want to overdo preparedness training, another type of drill that you may wish to consider is a *code red drill*. In a code red drill, a teacher or principal walks through the school, knocking loudly on classroom doors and saying, "Quick! Let me in! It's [STATE YOUR NAME], and I need your help!" If the students have been properly prepared, they'll resist the (very natural) temptation to open the door and try to help.

This type of drill is necessary because the teacher or principal could be under coercion by someone who wants to gain access to the classroom and cause harm. The students are instructed to report what's happened to their teacher who knows the current "safe word" a member of the faculty or staff would use during an emergency where someone's help was actually needed.

Focusing on culture and mission results in a twofold advantage when it comes to making schools safer. First, it leads to a community ethos that regards safety and security as important and where each member of the community assumes the responsibility of keeping every other member safe. Second, by addressing the questions of what makes the school distinctive, a focus on culture and mission helps administrators identify and address challenges that may be greater at their schools than they might be in other academic environments.

ACTIVE-SHOOTER SCENARIOS

Although school shootings are actually quite rare, the attention they receive in the media, along with the fear they instill in the hearts of students and their parents, makes them the safety issue that administrators are asked about most. The best approach to these questions is to be candid, noting that everyone at the school takes these situations very seriously, adopts security measures that minimize the risk of such an emergency, and discusses openly and honestly what students need to do in the event that the unthinkable happens.

If a school has a sign-in system requiring all visitors to wear badges or name tags, students should be told, in whatever manner is appropriate for their ages, that this action has been taken in order to keep them safe. They should be instructed to report to their teacher anytime they see a visitor on campus without a name tag regardless if they have seen the parent or guest in the school on previous occasions.

While school shootings can be random acts of violence, many of them do involve someone who's already known to the school community, such as a recently disciplined student, a parent who's angry at a teacher for whatever reason, a former employee who was terminated for cause, or a sibling of a current student who lives in a troubled domestic environment.

All members of the faculty, staff, and administration need to watch for the warning signs of potential violence, actions that are known as *gateway behaviors*. For example, has a parent sent threatening emails to the staff, been verbally abusive to their spouse or children, or become enraged (not just ordinarily angry or upset) because of a decision made by the school? Are they talking negatively about the school in ways that might be regarded as threats?

Gateway behaviors that could lead to acts of violence or self-harm are warning signs that school leaders *must* take seriously. If at any time you or any member of your staff feels vulnerable, you have to act. Your response could even go as far as not letting certain parents into your school out of a concern for the safety of those in the community. Of course, taking this action requires going through the proper legal channels, but it does remain an option.

School leaders today *have* to be vigilant. They have to be proactive in recognizing and addressing gateway behaviors. Some administrators hesitate to act because they're afraid of insulting a parent or member of the school community, but they have to remember that no one will ever blame a leader who takes the initiative in protecting his or her students. If you take action and are wrong, you may have a complaint filed against you to your board or superintendent, but if you are right and fail to act, the consequences are too terrible to imagine.

School leaders should also be proactive in training their teachers to look for warning signs on social media and in their students' work. Teachers should check periodically for gateway behaviors on websites that their students visit, texts and emails that students exchange, poetry and short stories turned in as assignments, and the drawings or doodles that students create.

Are they communicating in ways that indicate aggression or anger? Are they visiting websites that promote violence? Do the images that they create depict blood, gore, killing, or self-harm? If any of these gateway behaviors occur, the teachers should immediately contact their supervisor, who will then assign a mental health professional or guidance counselor to explore the situation.

Not all parents will respond rationally if they feel that their children have been "singled out" or "treated as though they were threats." But any levelheaded parent—not to mention any levelheaded superintendent or member of the school board—will appreciate that you have taken the safety of *all* the students seriously.

BULLYING

Bullying is the use of power or the perception of power for the purposes of intimidation. In a school setting, the power used by the bully often results from a difference in age, size, physical strength, or sheer aggressiveness. The website stopbullying.gov, which is sponsored by the United States federal government, notes that there are three primary forms of childhood bullying:

- *Verbal abuse*, which consists of teasing, name-calling, inappropriate sexual comments, taunting, or threatening to cause harm
- *Social or relational abuse*, which consists of hurting someone's reputation or relationships, leaving someone out of group activities on purpose, telling other students not to be friends with someone, spreading rumors about someone, or embarrassing someone in public
- *Physical abuse*, which consists of hurting someone's body or possessions, spitting on or toward someone, tripping or pushing, taking or damaging someone's possessions, or making mean or offensive hand gestures. (Adapted from stopbullying.gov 2018)

When teachers and administrators in many schools encounter instances of bullying, their first response is often to impose punishments on the bully in an effort to curb his or her inappropriate behavior. Unfortunately, these attempts at solutions usually backfire, *confirming* in the bully's mind the impression that an effective strategy for those in power is to inflict suffering on those in more vulnerable positions.

A second reason why punishment often fails to reduce bullying is that it ignores the domestic and psychological factors that may have produced the aggressive behavior in the first place. Many bullies may try to convey an attitude of high self-confidence, even haughtiness, but the primary reason why they strike at weaker students is that they have low self-esteem and are trying to compensate for their own social anxiety by attacking others before they themselves are attacked.

Other bullies may be acting inappropriately because of a variety of issues occurring at home, including domestic abuse, a lack of support and affection from their parents, or bullying behavior from their siblings.

A more effective strategy for combating bullying might begin with a community-wide discussion about bullying and its destructive effects that follows a movie like Lee Hirsch and Cynthia Lowen's *Bully* (2011), Diane Keaton, Dany Wolf, and J. T. LeRoy's *Elephant* (2003), Amy S. Weber, Danny Roth, and Jeffrey Spilman's *A Girl Like Her* (2015), or any other current film about bullying that conveys an appropriate message.

By seeing the impact of this behavior on people in a medium that students are familiar with, they can begin to develop greater empathy for the victims of bullying and refrain from behaviors that are not in accordance with community values.

For younger students, similar discussions about the dangers of bullying might occur following reading relevant stories in comic books or graphic novels, watching puppet shows, engaging in role-playing games, or listening to age-appropriate fictional accounts. Students can be asked questions about what the person in the story who was being bullied should have done, what his or her classmates should have done differently, and what a reasonable and constructive approach would have been that would have enabled the bully to make up for what he or she did and to become reintegrated into the community.

By teaching students techniques of conflict resolution that are both effective and appropriate, schools not only reduce the instances of bullying that occur among their students but also provide each student with a valuable lifelong skill.

Teachers and students alike become more alert to the types of antisocial behavior that might escalate into bullying, such as prolonged and angry stares at another student, turning one's back on another person, or simply pretending that that person doesn't exist. They learn to intervene early enough to resolve differences *before* anyone is actually bullied and thus create stronger, more empathetic communities.

Moreover, by demonstrating constructive behavior between one teacher and another or between an administrator and a teacher, we serve as good role models for our students about how adults are expected to act within a social context.

CYBERBULLYING

With one notable exception that will be considered below, most of the ways in which bullying can be addressed also apply to cyberbullying, the use of electronic media, such as text messages and social media sites, to intimidate or threaten others.

Cyberbullying is both similar to and different from traditional bullying. It's similar in the psychological and emotional impact it can have on the student who is bullied. It's different because aggressors often feel that they're protected by a perceived "wall of separation" from their victims that is provided by the electronic medium itself. Some students who could not bring themselves to bully another child face-to-face will not hesitate to bully another child online.

Nevertheless, there is one major difference in how instances of bullying and cyberbullying should be handled. Although punishments are rarely effective when traditional bullying occurs, research conducted by Sameer Hinduja and Justin Patchin, the codirectors of the Cyberbullying Research Center, suggests that students who clearly understand that cyberbullying will result in discipline are less likely to engage in this practice (Hinduja and Patchin 2018, 7).

As a result, Hinduja and Patchin recommend the following approaches to reducing the dangers on peer-on-peer cyberbullying in schools:

- Engage in regular discussion with students about what cyberbullying is, why it is harmful, how it is inconsistent with the values of the school community, and which types of sanctions may result if it occurs.
- If and when cyberbullying does occur, take steps to identify the student(s) responsible and react in a manner that is "commensurate with the harm done and the disruption that has occurred." (Hinduja and Patchin 2018, p. 7).
- For relatively minor incidents of cyberbullying, develop creative response strategies, such as requiring those responsible "to create anti-cyberbullying posters to be displayed throughout the school or a public service announcement (PSA) video conveying an anti-bullying and/or pro-kindness message" (Hinduja and Patchin 2018, p. 7).
- For more serious violations of anticyberbullying policies, these creative response strategies should be combined with calls to the aggressor's parents, counseling, and suspension of privileges.
- In truly severe cases, where it may be necessary to protect the victim of cyberbullying from further abuse or the perpetrator from retaliation, more serious consequences—such as detention, in-school or external suspension, reassignment of school placement, or expulsion—should be considered.

It should be remembered, too, that the *victims* of cyberbullying may well need counseling and further support since the experience may prove to have been even more traumatic for the victim than it initially appeared and might lead to challenges that arise only months or years later.

A CASE STUDY IN SAFETY AND SECURITY

Seymore Problems has just been appointed as principal of the Wrack and Ruin Academy. Upon his arrival, he observes a number of factors that cause him concern:

- The school is located in a known floodplain.
- Electrical sockets in many classrooms have numerous extension cords plugged into them.

- Several of these extension cords cross aisles where teachers and students walk every day.
- The school has eleven entry doors, all of which remain unlocked throughout the school day.
- Those entry doors are all indicated on the map of the school that appears on the school's website.
- That online map also identifies individual classrooms, locker rooms, science labs, and evacuation routes.
- There are student play areas on each side of the main access road used by buses and parents to transport students to and from school.
- Because Wrack and Ruin Academy is located in a small town that is considered safe, there is no sign-in procedure for visitors.
- The school is understaffed, so hallways are unmonitored.
- The school has no electronic alarm or closed-circuit television system.
- Fire drills are conducted once a week throughout the school year.
- There is no regular staff training on how to identify potential physical dangers or indications that students may be having behavioral or mental challenges.
- First aid kits are out of date and low on supplies.
- Numerous master keys have been distributed, and there is no list of who has them.
- Despite the fact that Wrack and Ruin Academy is fortunate in not having experienced any losses, injuries, or deaths due to unsafe conditions, students often report that they are anxious because their school is such a dangerous environment.

As Principal Problems reviews this list, he knows that he has his work cut out for him. But if you were to advise him on the most critical actions to take immediately, where should he begin in his effort to promote a more effective environment of school safety and security? What would you advise him to do as part of a longer-range plan?

DISCUSSION OF THE CASE STUDY

As always, form your own ideas about how to respond to this case study before reading the authors' suggestions. Once you have developed your answer, continue reading to see several ideas about what you might recommend.

Clearly all the issues that Principal Problems has identified are serious safety concerns that need to be addressed. But some of these problems can be handled immediately, while others will require some long-term planning. Among the issues that Principal Problems might address immediately are

- requiring that extension cords be removed from all classrooms and that no more than one device be connected to any one plug,
- locking all entry doors to the outside (while permitting them to be opened from the inside in case of emergency) and permitting entrance to the building through only a single, monitored access point,
- instituting a sign-in procedure with identification checks and time-limited identification badges to all visitors,
- reassigning staff responsibilities so that hallways are always monitored,
- removing all indication of entry doors, specific rooms, and evacuation points from the school's website because this information could be used by an intruder,
- relocating student play areas so that they are away from traffic lanes,
- if the budget allows, instituting electronic alarms and a closed-circuit television system. If the budget does not currently allow for these items, they should be made high priority items in the school's strategic plan and fundraising campaign,
- rescheduling emergency drills so that they are conducted once a month, with a regular rotation among drills devoted to evacuation, sheltering in place, and moving to safer quarters,
- resupplying and updating first aid kits, and
- rekeying the building and limiting the number of master keys to critical personnel only, with a continually updated list of who has these keys in their possession.

Then as part of the school's longer-range plans, Principal Problems might consider taking the following actions:

- Instituting regular community-wide discussions of the school's culture, mission, and values with the goal of promoting a community with a greater dedication to empathy, mutual support and protection, and safety
- Instituting periodic staff training on how to identify potential physical dangers or indications that students may be having behavioral or mental challenges
- Developing a comprehensive plan for dealing with the risks resulting from the school's location in a floodplain and incorporating response to floods into the school's schedule of emergency preparedness drills
- Developing a master plan for the school's physical plant with play areas, pedestrian paths, and vehicle traffic all located in separate zones so as to promote further safety
- Developing a plan for how the school will address the likely mental health problems and other challenges that may arise following an emergency

Based on your personal experience, you may have organized some of these actions differently. For example, you may have assumed that the school's budget could not immediately absorb costs related to electronic alarms, a closed-circuit television, resupplying first aid kits, or rekeying the entire building. The fact is that some schools are better funded than others or have greater flexibility in how resources may be allocated. Nevertheless, this exercise is a useful start for your own similar process in identifying potential problems and then developing both short-term and long-term plans to address those problems.

KEY POINTS IN THIS CHAPTER

- The issue of school safety involves creating learning environments that both are safe and feel safe.
- The single most important step in promoting safer schools is developing a school-wide culture of mutual responsibility and safety.
- In order to increase the safety and security of their schools, administrators need to *plan for what they can anticipate and prepare for what they can't.*
- Regular safety drills should occur roughly once a month and should include a variety of emergency responses: evacuation, sheltering in place, moving to safer quarters, and any other responses to additional challenges that may arise because of the school's unique location, programs, or mission.
- Bullying is usually best addressed through interventions that do not rely primarily on punishment.
- In the case of cyberbullying, however, students should be made aware of the sanctions that may be imposed on those who engage in this activity.
- All faculty and staff members should be trained in how to identify *gateway behaviors*: behaviors that indicate students are at risk for performing actions that might harm themselves or others.

REFERENCES

Cherry Creek School District #5. n.d. "Safety & Security Mission Statement." http://www.cherrycreekschools.org/Safety-and-Wellness/SafeSchools/Pages/default.aspx

Fein, R. A., B. Vossekuil, W. S. Pollack, R. Borum, W. Modzeleski, & M. Reddy. 2004. *Threat Assessment in Schools: A Guide to Managing Threatening Situations and to Creating Safe School Climates.* https://rems.ed.gov/docs/ThreatAssessmentinSchools.pdf

Fox, J. A., & E. E. Fridel. 2018. "The Three R's of School Shootings: Risk, Readiness, and Response." In *The Wiley Handbook on Violence in Education: Forms, Factors, and Preventions* edited by H. Shapiro, 15–36. New York, NY: Wiley-Blackwell.

Goldstein, D. 2018. "Why Campus Shootings Are so Shocking: School is the 'Safest Place' for a Child." *The New York Times*, May 22, 2018. https://www.nytimes.com/2018/05/22/us/safe-school-shootings.html

Hamblin, J. 2018. "What Are Active-Shooter Drills Doing to Kids?" *The Atlantic*, February 28, 2018. https://www.theatlantic.com/health/archive/2018/02/effects-of-active-shooter/554150/

Hiltzik, M. 2018. "Don't Be Misled by the Publicity on Shootings: For Kids, Schools Actually Are the Safest Refuges from Gun Violence." *Los Angeles Times*, March 16, 2018. http://www.latimes.com/business/hiltzik/la-fi-hiltzik-school-safety-20180316-story.html

Hinduja, S., & J. W. Patchin. 2018. *Cyberbullying Identification, Prevention, and Response.* Cyberbullying Research Center. https://cyberbullying.org/Cyberbullying-Identification-Prevention-Response-2018.pdf

Hirsch, L., & C. Lowen (Producers). *Bully.* Motion Picture. Directed by L. Hirsch. USA: Weinstein Company, Where We Live Films, EnhanceTV, & ABC2/KIDS. 2011.

Katsiyannis, A., D. K. Whitford, & R. P. Ennis. 2018. "Historical Examination of United States Intentional Mass School Shootings in the 20th and 21st Centuries: Implications for Students, Schools, and Society." *Journal of Child and Family Studies* 8(27): 2562–573.

Keaton, D., D. Wolf, & J. T. LeRoy (Producers). 2003. *Elephant.* Motion Picture. Directed by G. Van Sant. USA: First Line Features & HBO Films.

Malafronte, K. 2018. "School Lockdowns Could Have Psychological Effects on Children." *Campus Safety*, December 28, 2018. https://www.campussafetymagazine.com/safety/school-lockdowns-psychological-effects/

Ortiz, H. R. 2011. *Educational Facilities Vulnerability/Hazard Assessment Checklist.* https://rems.ed.gov/Docs/ACEF_ED_Facilitiesvulnerability-Hazardchecklist.pdf.

Perumean-Chaney, S. E., & L. M. Sutton. 2013. "Students and Perceived School Safety: The Impact of School Security Measures." *American Journal of Criminal Justice* 4(38): 570–88.

Rich, S., & J. W. Cox. 2018. "What if Someone Was Shooting?" *The Washington Post*, December 26, 2018. https://www.washingtonpost.com/graphics/2018/local/school-lockdowns-in-america/?noredirect=on&utm_term=.982ac4f1f1fd

Soft Lockdown: Definition. (2009.) *Arlington Heights, Illinois, Cardinal News.* https://www.arlingtoncardinal.com/2009/09/soft-lockdown/

Stopbullying.gov. 2018. https://www.stopbullying.gov/what-is-bullying/index.html.

Threat Assessment Template. 2016. Threat Assessment Template. www.doe.in.gov/sites/default/files/safety/template.docx

Toppo, G. 2013. "Schools Safe as Ever Despite Spate of Shootings, Scares." *USA Today*, November 13, 2013. https://www.usatoday.com/story/news/nation/2013/11/13/school-violence-security-sandy-hook/3446023/

Van Brunt, B. 2016. "Assessing Threat in Written Communications, Social Media, and Creative Writing." *Violence and Gender* 3(2): 78–88.

Weber, A. S., D. Roth, & J. Spilman (Producers). 2015. *A Girl Like Her.* Motion Picture. Directed by A. S. Weber. USA: Parkside Releasing.

Woods, R. (n.d.). *School Safety Assessment.* https://www.gadoe.org/Curriculum-Instruction-and-Assessment/Curriculum-and-Instruction/Documents/School%20Safety%20Assessment.pdf

RESOURCES

Brunner, J. M., & D. K. Lewis. 2009. *Safe and Secure Schools: 27 Strategies for Prevention and Intervention.* Thousand Oaks, CA: Corwin.

Trump, K. S. 2011. *Proactive School Security and Emergency Preparedness Planning* (2nd ed.). Thousand Oaks, CA: Corwin.

Van, D. J. 2011. *Assessing Student Threats: A Handbook for Implementing the Salem-Keizer System.* Lanham, MD: Rowman & Littlefield.

Chapter Three

Hiring for Excellence

Second only to keeping students and other members of the school community safe, hiring the right people is probably the most important task that school leaders have. If you hire for excellence, your efforts to create the kind of culture and mission that today's students deserve will become much easier. If you hire even one wrong person, the entire atmosphere of a school may change, and achieving your long-term goals can become nearly impossible.

Despite how important hiring the right people can be, most school systems and administrators engage in a practice that's ineffective, expensive, and unlikely to provide the results they hope to achieve. In order to understand why school leaders so often make hiring mistakes, let's engage in a brief thought experiment.

Suppose you have a friend who's about to get married and looking for the best possible baker for the wedding cake. When you ask your friend to describe the process used to select the baker, the answer you receive is, "Well, I have each baker come in for an appointment. Then I ask each baker to describe his or her philosophy of baking, to describe what he or she does when preparing a cake, and to tell me his or her strengths and weaknesses as a baker."

You'd probably conclude that your friend's process is ridiculous and not particularly useful in selecting the right baker. "Wouldn't it be simpler just to taste samples of their work? Then you can decide very easily which ones you like and which ones you don't like. After all, what bakers *say* they do when they prepare wedding cakes and what they actually do once they're in the kitchen may not be the same. It's both easier and more effective to evaluate a baker's results when you want to discover excellence than to talk with them about their philosophy and process."

This brief thought experiment highlights the major problem with how most members of the faculty and staff are selected. They're *interviewed*, not required to *demonstrate effective behaviors* or provide *evidence of effectiveness*.

So, if school leaders want to increase the likelihood that they'll be able to hire for excellence, they have to begin the practice of *talking less and observing more*. Nearly anyone can pretend to be a good teacher for the duration of the typical interview, but requiring that people actually do what they say they can do helps distinguish between those who merely have the right answers and those who demonstrate the right skills.

Before hiring anyone for a faculty or staff position, effective school leaders start by drawing up two lists: one that outlines all of the critical functions that the teacher will have to perform and one that outlines many of the "value-added" contributions that would be highly desirable but not absolutely essential to have. The next step is a matter of asking, "What would I need to observe in order to make certain that a candidate can perform all the critical functions on my first list?"

Let's suppose that you're hiring a new second-grade teacher who will be required to teach all academic areas. Your list of critical functions might include the following:

- Develop suitable lesson plans for students demonstrating a wide range of academic needs and levels of performance.
- Execute the lesson plans developed, adapting them according to individual student need and ability.
- Manage classroom behavior and address typical behavioral challenges at the second-grade level.
- Evaluate student work effectively and provide appropriate, constructive advice.
- Evaluate each student's ability to communicate with others and to work in groups, providing appropriate feedback as necessary.
- Assign and evaluate suitable amounts and types of homework.
- Administer and evaluate examinations that meet all current state and local standards for subjects.
- Prepare students for standardized tests that meet all state and local requirements, and provide diagnostic feedback, as necessary.
- Understand the curricular goals of grades one and three in order to build on students' past accomplishments and better prepare them for future opportunities.
- Adhere to all school policies, as well as policies at the system, state, and national level.
- Conduct conferences with parents and guardians.
- Provide recommendations on textbooks, as needed.

- Serve as a good role model.
- Act as a collegial and supportive member of the school community.

Once this list is created, the next question becomes, "What would I need to observe in order to be certain that a candidate can meet all these requirements?"

Approached from this perspective, the interview process for a prospective teacher becomes less a series of questions to be answered and more a series of competencies to generate. It's not at all uncommon in traditional interviews for candidates to teach all or part of a class so that their demeanor can be observed. But all too often those observations are rather limited. There's very little opportunity to evaluate how the teacher performs with a full range of students who might have very different levels of academic performance and demonstrate several types of behavioral challenges.

A better strategy is, therefore, to witness each prospective teacher in as many environments as possible that are similar to those that he or she will actually experience on the job. How does the candidate interact with very bright students who grasp concepts immediately? How does he or she interact with those who have far more trouble understanding? And how does that teacher interact with the vast majority of the students who fall somewhere between those two extremes?

How does the candidate act in a meeting with other teachers when emotions are running high and differences of opinion are pronounced? How does the candidate set priorities on days when the demands are many and the opportunities for reflection very few? (On strategies for evaluating work samples submitted by candidates for teaching positions, see Rose, English, and Finney 2014, pp. 85–102.)

Of course, it's not always possible to evaluate prospective teachers under all these conditions. Often teachers have to be hired on very short notice or during vacation periods when students aren't available. In these situations, you may still be able to learn something about the candidate's likely behavior on the job by setting up several different kinds of mock classes that he or she has to teach, with current teachers acting as "students." It may also be necessary to have each candidate role-play a situation, such as dealing with a rude student, difficult colleague, helicopter parent (see chapter 8), or overly demanding supervisor.

If none of those options are available, at least be sure to ask more probing questions of the candidate's references about how he or she responded to various types of situations. Possible questions or prompts include the following:

- What is [THE CANDIDATE] like when frustrated, angry, or annoyed?

- Describe a situation in which [THE CANDIDATE]'s ideas were opposed or rejected by others. How did [THE CANDIDATE] respond?
- Describe what [THE CANDIDATE] was like when you saw his or her behavior at its worst.

When you're screening for candidates who are likely to become cooperative and supportive colleagues, it's not good enough to ask them about their degree of collegiality. Every candidate, even the most destructive and self-centered ones, know how to act collegial for the duration of an interview and to say they support teamwork and consensus building. Instead of asking about collegiality, watch a candidate's body language when he or she interacts with other members of the faculty and staff.

Even better, watch how the candidate interacts with those whom he or she might regard as "insignificant," such as custodians and members of the wait-staff when you go out to lunch. Those are the people with whom candidates are likely to act more naturally because, in their minds, "they don't matter in terms of whether I get this job." But make no mistake about it: how candidates treat maintenance workers and servers today is a good indication of how they'll be treating their coworkers tomorrow.

Once you've determined that a candidate can meet (or easily learn to meet) all the requirements on your first list, you can begin to look for the "value-added" attributes on your second list. For example, you might describe the following as "nice to have but not essential" characteristics:

- Knowledge of accreditation policies and experience in writing the reports required by accrediting bodies
- Skill at developing new policies
- A calm and comfortable manner when speaking to groups of parents and other external stakeholders
- Leadership potential
- The ability to further diversify the faculty
- A talent for critiquing current practices in a constructive manner and recommending more effective alternatives

Since you already know which of your candidates have the abilities that you regard as critical, you can now begin to select the best among them by using these additional criteria. To return to our example of choosing a baker for a wedding cake, you already know which chef produces cakes that are delicious and attractive; you can now begin to focus on the ones that are willing to negotiate their rates and waive the delivery fee.

In the case of actual candidates for teaching positions, your thought process might be something like the following: "Of the four candidates I interviewed, two have demonstrated that they have everything I'm looking for in terms of abilities and attributes. One of the two will increase the diversity of our staff and be able to help us with that self-study we've got coming up in a year. The other has experience in community outreach. All of that is desirable, but diversity and accreditation are both mentioned on my list of preferred qualities, so I think I'll go with that candidate."

WHERE DO THE BEST CANDIDATES COME FROM?

At this point, some readers might be thinking, "All of that sounds well and good, but I have to work in the real world. My typical candidate pool doesn't always give me a choice of several stellar candidates to select from. Sometimes I'm lucky to find even one qualified candidate. So where are all these wonderful candidates supposed to come from?"

In order to answer this question, we need to switch metaphors from cake baking to professional athletics. Suppose you have another friend who informs you that he or she just became the owner of a professional football team. "Congratulations!" you say. "How are you going to recruit the sort of players who are going to be able to win the Super Bowl?"

"Oh, you know," your friend replies. "I'll put an ad in the paper, see who applies, and choose the best athletes from among the applicants." If that's your friend's plan, you probably shouldn't plan on his or her team making it to the Super Bowl (or even making it to the playoffs) anytime soon. That's not how winning NFL teams hire their players. They identify the best players, no matter where they are, and go after them to recruit them. And that's exactly the same strategy successful school leaders use to recruit their academic "teams."

Following this strategy is a lot easier and less expensive than many school leaders believe. With the ubiquity of social media in people's lives, a message on LinkedIn, Facebook, and Twitter can bring you far better applications than a posting in the local newspaper or on the state employment job site. Get the word out that you're looking for "an award-winning high school biology teacher" or "a star teacher for the first grade who's also a reading specialist," and you'll attract applications you might not have received otherwise.

If you do happen to have at least a small budget available, posting a position on online job sites like Monster, Glassdoor, and Indeed can advertise it to an even broader range of highly qualified candidates. (For more on where and how to recruit excellent candidates, see Clement 2015, pp. 10–14.)

Another objection might arise. "Even if I do that, there's no way that I'll attract a candidate of national distinction to our school. We're simply too small/underfunded/remote/obscure/inner-city/[INSERT OTHER EXCUSE OF YOUR CHOICE] to be able to hire the best."

If you find yourself thinking thoughts of that sort, it's important to remember two things. First, most people don't decide to become teachers because they think it will bring them a high income and an easy life. *People become teachers because they want to make a positive difference in the world.* So, your job in reaching out to potential applicants is to make it clear that this position is one in which the applicant can truly make a difference. If you do that, the most committed applicants (in other words, exactly the type of people you want at your school) will come flocking to your door.

Second, remember that the interview process always goes two ways. At the same time that you're trying to decide whether a candidate is the right person for the job, your candidates are trying to decide whether the job is the right opportunity for them. So, don't just sit back and expect an applicant to wow you; take the initiative to wow your candidates. Write your job descriptions in such a way that people will *want* to apply for them. Reflect on the best features of your school and its location and highlight those. Make it clear that your job is one that an applicant will desperately *want* to have.

Imagine that you are a middle school language arts teacher who is considering applying for a new position. You look at a job site and see three positions available. The opening line of each position is as follows:

Position A. "Full-time language arts position available at Mountain Valley Middle School."

Position B. "You have the opportunity to be in on the ground floor of a new way of teaching language arts: Come make a difference with us!"

Position C. "Imagine teaching and living in a community of towering pines, gently flowing streams, and the friendliest people north of the Rio Grande."

Which of these jobs would be the first to interest you in applying? Which has the least impact initially? And yet which of them is like the vast majority of the job postings you see in education?

Most people who answer these questions are likely to say that either Position B or Position C sounds much more appealing and inviting than the first position. They allow applicants to envision themselves working at that school and being a part of an enterprise that would be important, exciting, or both. And yet, the vast majority of job announcements today begin with a statement similar to that in Position A. In an effort to be professional (or perhaps because the author is merely imitating other job postings), every element of interest, personality, and style ends up being removed.

Let's explore a way of writing job announcements that will make the best candidates actually *want* to apply. Imagine the candidate pool a school leader might attract with the following notice placed on LinkedIn and other appropriate social media sites.

The Chester A. Arthur Academy, a future-focused high school located in East Palm Beach, Florida, is recruiting rock star teachers with master's degrees and a passion to work with tomorrow's leaders. The Academy is actively seeking teachers who believe they can unleash the full potential of each of their students, create a learning environment that fosters critical thinking, creativity, and social responsibility, and at the same time instill a joy for learning. If you would like to be part of a team of educators that will play a role in shaping those who will change our world, please contact us at carthur@chesteraarthurschool.edu.
#education #florida #criticalthinking #creativity #socialresponsibility #leadership

Phrased in this way, the announcement isn't about a job; it's about a calling, and it's thus likely to attract applicants who are driven by mission at least as much as they're driven by salary and benefits. Notice, too, how the choice of hashtags not only reinforces the message of the announcement but also makes it easier for potential teachers to find the advertisement.

The fact is that school leaders often don't do enough to make the best possible candidates *want* to apply for their jobs. They don't reflect enough on what makes their schools and communities unique and desirable. They don't *sell* their positions hard enough to attract the applicants who will help them build the school to its greatest potential.

So, before you write your next job posting, reflect on what it is that should make someone eager to take your job. Then lead your posting with that, not the sort of details that are better left for later. Remember that if you don't attract the right candidates with the first line of your job posting, they'll never read the second line.

WHAT DO I LOOK FOR IN THE APPLICATIONS I RECEIVE?

Once you start receiving applications because of your outreach on social media and the creativity of your job posting, it's time to screen the applications into three categories: highly competitive, competitive, and noncompetitive.

The last two categories are the easiest to understand: Competitive candidates meet your absolute requirements; noncompetitive candidates don't. But it can be harder to determine what makes a given candidate highly competitive.

Certainly a highly competitive candidate will meet, even exceed, your basic requirements. But they will also bring something extra that the merely competitive candidates don't have. Perhaps they'll possess some of those "value-added" attributes that were discussed earlier. Perhaps they'll demonstrate a certain flair for creativity that would make your school even better than it already is. Perhaps they have additional skills that, although you don't need them right now, might be useful in the future.

Your qualifications for including someone in the highly competitive category will depend on your precise needs and situation, but it's the category where you're most likely to find your school's next superstar.

At the same time, you also want to be on the lookout for certain warning signs that might appear in applications. One of the biggest red flags that many school leaders miss is the indication that someone might be a "school hopper," someone who moves from school to school every two or three years.

If you talk to such an applicant, he or she is likely to have very compelling reasons for why these frequent changes of job were necessary: there were challenges that arose in his or her personal life; the school administration wasn't supportive; it just wasn't the right fit; and so on. But as legitimate as those reasons may sound, you are justified in remaining a bit skeptical. Why? Primarily because teachers want and need to find a school that they can call home. A school shouldn't just be a place where they collect a paycheck; it should also be a community that they become more attached to over time, a place where they can make a difference because of their long-term commitment. A school hopper can't commit. He or she won't be a team player regardless of whatever is said at the interview.

School leaders need to be particularly wary of the candidate who always seems to end up in environments where the administration was incompetent and other teachers were uncollegial. Anyone may end up in a situation like that once or perhaps twice over the course of an entire career, but if it happens to someone repeatedly, heed the warning signs: The only common denominator in a lengthy series of unfortunate placements is the school hopper himself or herself. Your goal is to develop a caring, professional, and committed school culture, and school hoppers won't enable you to reach that goal.

If you follow this advice, you know two things about those who remain in your highly competitive pool: they can perform all the required responsibilities of the jobs, and they are capable of long-term commitment. (The latter qualification also means that they are probably good colleagues. Someone *wanted* them to make a long-term commitment and so was willing to renew their contract.)

But even this information isn't enough to let you know whether a particular candidate is someone you should interview. The next factor school leaders should screen for is whether a candidate is a *problem solver* or a *problem seeker*.

A problem seeker is someone who will always complain, blame, or find fault with others. As has often been said (in a quotation widely misattributed to Albert Einstein), "Stay away from negative people. They have a problem for every solution." Problem seekers are toxic to the type of school culture you want to build. They may have great depth of knowledge and a host of professional accomplishments, but their negative attitude will almost certainly create an environment that drives away other employees and makes it harder for students of all ability levels to succeed.

Moreover, it's easier to discover who's a problem solver and who's a problem seeker than you may imagine. You start by looking at each candidate's social media activity. Do they post about having just had the worst workday ever? Do they do so repeatedly? If so, keep in mind that they're likely to make similar posts in the future and, that time, it will be about your students, their colleagues, and possibly you. Do they post online about how things always go wrong for them? Do they complain, even in jest, about their spouse?

If they do any of these things online, these are signs that the person is a problem seeker, and you'll be well advised to remove that person from your highly competitive pool. There are other excellent candidates out there; problem seekers are not worth the complications they inevitably bring with them.

WHAT DO YOU DO WHEN YOU *HAVE* TO INTERVIEW CANDIDATES?

When you've prescreened the applications so that you have the number remaining in your highly competitive pool that you want to meet in person, it's time to initiate the interview process. Remember what we saw earlier. The best interviews are those that contain less talking and more demonstrating. In the best of all possible worlds you want to *see* what your finalists can do.

But sometimes that's just not possible. Time constraints may mean that you only have a single day to interview all three or four of your finalists, and that's just not enough time to create as many sample teaching environments as you need to make an informed decision. Or perhaps you're conducting last-minute interviews over a time when school is not in session, and there aren't even enough members of the faculty and staff around to create a meaningful mock class. Or perhaps your system or supervisor isn't creative enough to allow you to engage in the type of behavior-based interviewing that was recommended earlier. Then what do you do?

When, for whatever reason, you *have* to interview candidates, you goal should be to ask questions that are as behavior-based as possible. Every candidate in the world knows how to dodge a question like, "What's your greatest weakness?" (The candidate tries to make a strength sound like a weakness: "Sometimes I just care about my students too much.") or "How would you describe your work style? ("I'm a team player and consensus builder.") So, ask questions that both are unexpected and require the person to describe actual past experiences or to imagine themselves responding to realistic situations. Then watch the candidate for *how* he or she answers at least as much as you watch for *what he or she says.*

Behavior-based prompts are those that begin with phrases like the following:

- Tell me about a when time . . . .
- Describe a possible situation where . . . .
- What were you thinking when you . . . ?
- Guide me through your decision-making process when you . . . .

By phrasing your question in this way, you gain better insight into both what a candidate actually did in a specific situation and (more important) *why* he or she did it. If the candidate cannot think of a situation similar to the one you're describing, then pose a hypothetical situation and ask the candidate to guide you through his or her thought processes. These behavior-based questions are much more effective than universal or theoretical questions in alerting you to how the person is likely to act once he or she becomes a member of your team.

In general, good behavioral interview questions don't have a single right or wrong answer. The goal is to determine the candidate's thought process, not to trap the candidate into making a mistake he or she couldn't possibly have foreseen. For this reason, questions about specific scenarios are good, but those scenarios shouldn't be so unique to your school or system that they put an external candidate at a disadvantage.

In addition to these behavior-based questions, there are a number of other questions you can ask that are far more revealing than the typical "How would you describe your teaching style?" or "Where do you see yourself in the next five years?" Here are a few examples of better questions to ask and what to look out for.

- *Who were your three most memorable students? What made them memorable?* Unless the candidate is a highly inexperienced teacher, one warning sign is if he or she can't even recall three specific students. It indicates that the person is not thoroughly engaged as a teacher and thus is unlikely to become a thoroughly engaged member of your community. A good answer to this question should be specific and, where possible, should reflect a range of student backgrounds or ability levels. Teachers who only recall their star pupils or those who are just like them may not be providing the level of support that can help less capable students or those of different ethnicities and economic backgrounds flourish.
- *Tell me about a time you had a confrontation with a coworker or a parent. What was the problem, and how did you solve it?* The goal with this

question is to see if the candidate is balanced and reasonable in his or her approach. If the answer is, "Oh! There have been so many. How can I choose just one?" you probably are interviewing a problem seeker, not a problem solver. As we saw earlier, the only common denominator in a series of difficult encounters with the candidate is the candidate himself or herself. On the other hand, if the candidate's answer is, "I never have any difficulties with my coworkers or parents. Everything always goes so smoothly," you'll want to probe more deeply. Any workplace is an environment where interpersonal difficulties arise, and the challenging environment of a school is no different. Keep probing until the candidate can identify a specific situation that allows you to evaluate the person's skills at communication and critical thinking.

- *How do you set priorities for your time since there are so many demands on you as a teacher?* This question is an excellent example of an inquiry that has no single correct answer. It is an insight into how the candidate thinks, not the specific conclusions that he or she draws. If you disagree with the candidate's specific priorities, you can always help correct those later (provided, of course, that the candidate is superb in all other ways), as long as his or her thought processes are reasonable.

- *We have three constituencies we work with on a daily basis. We have our peers, parents, and pupils. If I were to ask each group to share one adjective that would describe you, what would they say?* The goal with this question is to determine how self-aware the candidate is. If the candidate has to think too long about this question, he or she is either being humble or is not particularly mindful of the effect he or she has on others. You'll be able to recognize humility if the candidate, after a pause, says something like, "I just find it very difficult to talk about myself. I don't like to brag. I prefer to showcase my students' achievements. But if I had to guess, I imagine that what people would say is that I'm . . . ." You're hoping that the candidate will include such terms as *empathetic, kind, compassionate, considerate, creative, intelligent, funny, flexible, enthusiastic, perceptive,* and *a team player*. (On the personal traits that are most commonly signs of effective teachers, see McEwan-Adkins 2010, pp. 25–44.) It should be a warning sign if the candidate can't think of anything to say at all or uses words like *structured, always in control,* or *competitive*. Regardless of how the candidates describe themselves, however, always ask them to provide several specific examples of instances when they demonstrated that quality. For example, if a candidate says, "I believe they'd say I'm a self-starter who takes responsibility for what I do and who is highly resourceful," you'll want evidence that those words didn't merely come from a thesaurus or a book on good answers to interview questions. Ask for a specific case in which that quality was demonstrated. Then ask for another. Candidates often expect to be asked for a single example; they rarely have prepared answers about two or three specific instances. You'll know that a candidate is not particularly self-aware if he or she has to keep circling back to the same example to demonstrate the positive qualities he or she claims to have. Also, it is often perfectly acceptable for teachers to describe themselves as strict as long as they follow that term with the phrase "but fair." Many school leaders would, however, prefer that applicants for pre-K to eighth-grade positions emphasize their compassion and student-centeredness, leaving discussions of rigor and strict classroom management for those seeking high school positions.

- *Describe your colleagues from your last position.* This prompt is another insight into how the candidate views coworkers. Remember that if the candidate is negative about current colleagues, he or she is likely to regard future colleagues in much the same way.
- *If you were to look back on a meeting and think, "Now, that was a great meeting," what is likely to have brought you to that conclusion?* Meetings are the bane of a teacher's life, but little can be accomplished without them. By asking this question, you're looking for insight into the candidate's ability to distinguish between a productive meeting and one that simply wastes people's time. Since every meeting takes teachers away from activities that could benefit their students, you'll want coworkers who can recognize when a meeting is worthwhile and when the time of those in attendance would be better spent elsewhere.
- *If your supervisor assigned you a service task that you personally thought was not the best use of your time, what would you do?* This question helps you gain a sense of how this candidate views supervisor/employee relationships. Great schools tend to be staffed by teachers who speak their minds but who also realize that they can't always get their own way. You wouldn't want an employee who resented you (and probably his or her colleagues as well) because of being assigned a service task that could have been better accomplished in a different way. At the same time, you wouldn't want an employee who challenged every decision and felt it appropriate to "get in your face" about differences of opinion. So, you are looking for middle ground in this answer, something along the lines of, "I would certainly mention my concerns to my supervisor and hope that he or she might understand my point of view. But if my supervisor said that this service assignment was the best use of my time at the moment, I would do it. After all, we all need to be team players."
- *What have I forgotten to ask you?* Candidates frequently have skills and accomplishments that may not appear in their written materials but that they want us to know about. By asking this question, we give candidates a chance to highlight those items and provide us with important information that we may not have obtained otherwise.

- *What would you like to ask me?* Every excellent candidate should always have questions for us in an interview. If they don't, it's probably not a sign (despite what the candidate might say) that we've already covered every issue of significance to a future employee. More likely it means that the person isn't sufficiently invested in the job, hasn't done enough home-work about the school, or both. It should always be a warning sign when candidates have nothing they want to ask us about.

Over time, school leaders always develop their own key questions to ask, and undoubtedly you'll develop your own interview questions as well.

The important thing to remember, however, is that *how* a candidate chooses to answer a question is at least as important as *what* the candidate says. Be on the lookout for answers that suggest the candidate is collegial, forward thinking, and interested in solving problems, not merely identifying them. (For more ideas on how to develop behavior-based interview questions, see Clement 2008, pp. 37–60. For other types and examples of effective interview techniques, see Buller 2017a, pp. 91--113 and Buller 2017b, pp. 29–39.)

A CASE STUDY IN HIRING FOR EXCELLENCE

Imagine that you are Joy Tudaworld, the principal of Barren Valley Grove High School in Desert Shores, East Carolina. You are currently in need of a new English teacher, primarily for first- and second-year students who have demonstrated some difficulty in reading. If the candidate could also coach cheerleading, girls' volleyball, or golf, that would be a value-added component of the candidate's portfolio. One of your applicants is Yul B. Saury. A few selected passages of his application letter and résumé are below. Identify all the warning signs that would make you hesitant to interview this candidate.

Principle
Baren Graves High School
Desert Shores, EC

To Whom It May Concern:

I am applying for your English teacher job. I have many years experience teaching English. I am well regarded by my piers for my structured approach to teaching and my highly competitive spirit. (I try always to have my classes score better on exams than other teachers.)

I am available for an interview at any time. I hope to hear from you soon.

See you soon (I hope),
Yul B. Saury

SELECTIONS FROM THE RÉSUMÉ OF YUL B. SAURY

Experience

Hillsborough Springs Middle School, one year. Reason for leaving: Unsupportive administration.

Prairie Mountain Lakes High School, one and a half years. Reason for leaving: Rude, envious colleagues.

Fry cook at Quickie Takes Fast Food, two years. Reason for leaving: Found better job.

Hanover Grange School (substitute teacher), one year. Reason for leaving: Incapable students.

Strengths

Leadership
People-person
Highly organized

Weaknesses

None

DISCUSSION OF THE CASE STUDY

As with all case studies in this book, remember to have formulated your own answers before reading the authors' suggestions below. Once you've created you own list, see if it includes the following warning signs:

- Since you're hiring an English teacher, you may not want to consider a candidate who spells the words *principal* and *peers* incorrectly and who has been careless enough to get the name of your school wrong.
- While it is a matter of personal preference, many school leaders regard job application letters that begin with the phrase, "To Whom It May Concern," as indicative of the fact that the candidate has not even inquired enough into the school to learn the principal's name.
- Every sentence in the candidate's letter begins with the word *I*. Regardless of whether that practice is an indication of egotism or poor writing habits, you probably don't want such a person teaching English at your school.

- Other sentences have grammatical or stylistic problems, such as the lack of parallelism in the sentence, "I try always to have my classes score better on exams than other teachers."
- The candidate uses two terms of self-description that are themselves warning signs: *structured* and *competitive.*
- The closing of the candidate's application letter is overly familiar for professional writing and merely repeats the previous sentence.
- In the candidate's résumé, it is clear that he is a school hopper. In addition, the longest job he has held appears to have been an entry-level position unrelated to teaching.
- The reasons the candidate mentions for leaving previous jobs are usually other people's fault, except when he says that he found a better job. Those factors would appear to indicate that he is a problem seeker who tends to blame others when things go wrong and that he is not committed to any position he holds.
- The candidate claims to have strengths that are not validated by any of the information contained in either the cover letter or résumé.
- The candidate claims to have no weaknesses, a sign of either egotism, lack of self-awareness, or both.

KEY POINTS IN THIS CHAPTER

Best practices in hiring for excellence consist of

- observing behavior rather than simply asking questions,
- deciding in advance which qualities, abilities, and attributes in a candidate are essential and which are mere preferences (or value-added factors),
- recruiting excellent applicants rather than expecting them to find you,
- selling your school to potential applicants to make them *want* to apply,
- reviewing applications to determine which candidates are school hoppers and which are problem seekers,
- examining a candidate's social media trail in order to gain as much insight into each candidate's character as possible, and
- making questions as behavior-based as possible if traditional interviews are absolutely necessary.

REFERENCES

Buller, J. L. 2017a. *Best Practices for Faculty Search Committees: How to Review Applications and Interview Candidates.* San Francisco, CA: Jossey-Bass.
Buller, J. L. 2017b. *Hire the Right Faculty Member Every Time: Best Practices in Recruiting, Selecting, and Onboarding College Professors.* Lanham, MD: Rowman & Littlefield.

Clement, M. C. 2015. *10 Steps for Hiring Effective Teachers*. Thousand Oaks, CA: Corwin/ SAGE.

Clement, M. C. 2008. *Recruiting and Hiring Effective Teachers: A Behavior-Based Approach*. Alexandria, VA: Educational Research Service.

McEwan-Adkins, E. K. 2010. *10 Traits of Highly Effective Teachers: How to Hire, Coach, and Mentor Successful Teachers*. Moorabbin, Australia: Hawker Brownlow Education.

Rose, D. S., A. English., & T. G. Finney. 2014. *Hire Better Teachers Now: Using the Science of Selection to Find the Best Teachers for Your School*. Cambridge, MA: Harvard Education.

RESOURCES

Clement, M. C. 2016. *Retaining Effective Teachers: A Guide for Hiring, Induction, and Support*. Lanham, MD: Rowman & Littlefield.

Daresh, J. C., & B. N. Daresh. 2013. *How to Interview, Hire, and Retain High-Quality New Teachers* (3rd ed.). Bloomington, IN: Solution Tree.

Heller, D. A. 2004. *Teachers Wanted: Attracting and Retaining Good Teachers*. Alexandria, VA: Association for Supervision and Curriculum Development.

Hindman, J. L. 2014. *Effective Teacher Interviews: How Do I Hire Good Teachers?* Alexandria, VA: ASCD.

Kersten, T. A., & M. E. Clauson. 2015. *Personnel Priorities in Schools Today: Hiring, Supervising, and Evaluating Teachers*. Lanham, MD: Rowman & Littlefield.

Loeb, S., D. Kalogrides, & T. Béteille. 2011. *Effective Schools: Teacher Hiring, Assignment, Development, and Retention*. Cambridge, MA: National Bureau of Economic Research.

Rockoff, J. E. 2008. *Can You Recognize an Effective Teacher When You Recruit One?* Cambridge, MA: National Bureau of Economic Research.

Sleeter, C. E., L. V. I. Neal, & K. K. Kumashiro (eds.). 2015. *Diversifying the Teacher Workforce: Preparing and Retaining Highly Effective Teachers*. New York, NY: Routledge.

Chapter Four

Faculty and Staff Evaluation

The evaluation of the faculty and staff is one of a school leader's most important responsibilities. It's also likely to be one of his or her least favorite. Evaluation is important because it gives school leaders a chance to review with employees what went well (and so should continue and perhaps be expanded in the future), what didn't go as well as it should have (and so should be changed), and how each person's performance aligns with the mission and culture of the school. It's unpleasant because it can be awkward, occupies an incredible amount of time, leads to confrontations, and often doesn't accomplish the goals it sets out to achieve.

The notion that faculty and staff evaluation isn't particularly effective doesn't merely reflect the opinion of many school leaders; it is a fact widely known by human resource professionals, and it has been documented repeatedly in studies. In a 2007 study, management consultant Fred Nickols identified a wide range of problems with the ways in which employee appraisals are typically performed:

- They tend to "assess the assessable," focusing on goals and metrics that are easily quantified instead of those that are really important.
- They frequently focus on what the person did wrong instead of what the person did right, resulting in negative feelings on the part of the employee.
- They stress individual performance even though a great deal of success in the modern workplace is team based.
- They emphasize tasks completed rather than the overall process and mission, resulting in a short-term view.
- They are highly subjective, and their success depends a great deal on the skill of the supervisor in conducting evaluations, often reducing them to little more than political game playing.

- They are expensive if done correctly, meaning that many organizations economize by using a poorly designed process that does not lead to better training and includes no adequate mechanism for appeals.

Because of all these flaws, too many supervisors simply go through the motions when conducting employee evaluations. As the author of *Management Rewired* (2009), Charles S. Jacobs has noted, "Some liken the annual performance appraisal to a root canal, but I think it's much more like Japanese Kabuki theater. The actors in this ritual go through predetermined stylized motions, and it's often hard to find any direct connection to reality" (Jacobs 2010).

As many people who conduct employee evaluations can attest, good employees tend to react badly to criticism. They're so concerned about doing a good job that they'll fixate on the one corrective activity that a manager recommends instead of the dozen of positive things said during the evaluation. Poor employees, on the other hand, tend to be indifferent to criticism. That is, in fact, *why* they're poor employees.

As troubling as these results may be in most lines of work, the challenges to effective evaluation are even more difficult for school leaders. In an educational setting, administrators have few rewards or penalties that they can couple with the annual performance appraisal.

Profit sharing and year-end bonuses simply don't exist in the educational environment, and contracts, system bureaucracy, and tenure can make dismissing an ineffective teacher far more difficult than it is for a company to terminate a poor employee. Moreover, school leaders are rarely not trained in how to do faculty and staff evaluations effectively. As a result, they frequently just "go through the motions," trying to get them done as quickly as possible.

KEYS TO BETTER EVALUATIONS

Many systems used to evaluate members of the faculty and staff are based on false assumptions. Perhaps the most destructive of these false assumptions is that the employees of a school constitute a *random distribution*. If you were to take up a position along a city street where people passed by in large numbers all day, many aspects of the population you'd encounter would represent a random population in certain respects.

For example, if you measured each person's height and plotted that information on a graph, you'd end up with data that reflected the familiar bell-shaped curve. Relatively few people would be very tall or very short; a great many people would be at a height that fell at roughly the middle of your graph; and, as you moved from either end of the graph toward the middle, the number of people at that height would rise exponentially.

In the evaluation systems used by many schools, the expectation is that faculty and staff performance will reflect this same kind of random distribution. Relatively few people would perform either very well or very poorly; a great many people would perform at a satisfactory level; and, as you moved from either end of the graph toward the middle, the number of people who performed at that level would rise exponentially. In fact, forcing results to fit this predictive model is *required* in some systems. In order for one employee to be rated as *excellent*, another employee has to be rated as *not meeting expectations*, and so on.

But *school employees are not a random population*. They have to be trained, certified, or credentialed. They have to pass background checks. They are only hired after an interview process—which, if you follow the guidelines recommended in the previous chapter, will be quite rigorous—and they have probably improved their skills as the result of in-service training and other evaluation processes.

For all of these reasons, if an evaluation system is truly objective, *the population of school employees skews toward excellent* and does not reflect a standard bell-shaped curve in terms of performance. To force the results of an evaluation process to follow such a curve means to rank many members of the faculty and staff as less effective than they actually are.

So, how are school leaders able to conduct evaluations that set high standards for performance while also respecting members of the faculty and staff as professionals who often don't need a "boss" to define for them what excellence means in an educational setting? In order to begin answering this question, school leaders should remember a lesson they themselves learned when they were studying to become teachers: *not all types of evaluations are alike.*

Consider, for example, how educators evaluate their students.

- Some evaluations are *diagnostic*. They provide us with baseline information so that teachers can better adapt their pedagogical approaches to the students' needs. For this reason, a transfer student might be given a math placement exam or a foreign language placement exam in order to make sure that the student is registered in a course that neither repeats what he or she has already learned nor is much too difficult.
- Some evaluations are *formative*. They tell us where the student is having difficulty so that the teacher can remediate the problem.
- Some evaluations are *summative*. They tell the school whether the student has reached a certain goal, such as qualifying to be advanced to the next grade or to graduate from the program entirely.

- And some evaluations are *summative-formative*. They allow the school to make a summative decision ("You will be promoted to the next grade level . . .") while at the same time leading to a formative plan (". . . but you will need to complete a summer session in order to bring your reading skills up to the required standard.")

This distinction in types of evaluation, which teachers understand completely when it comes to their students, is sometimes overlooked when administrators conduct their own evaluations of teachers. The school leaders may act on the assumption that every employee evaluation is either summative or summative-formative; it needs always to result in some decision, such as whether the teacher's contract will be renewed or whether the staff member will receive an increase in salary.

But, like their students, teachers also benefit from diagnostic and formative evaluation. With more diagnostic evaluation, the strengths of teachers and staff members can better be used for helping the school fulfill its mission, and the challenges of teachers and staff members can better be overcome through professional development and in-service training. With more formative evaluation, teachers and staff members come to regard administrators as mentors and coaches who want to ensure their success rather than as judges and critics who want to catch them doing something wrong.

Formative and summative-formative evaluations require school leaders not simply to look at the past and appraise what happened but also to look toward the future and set meaningful goals for the person who is being evaluated.

Just as good teachers use rubrics not only to ensure fair evaluation of student work but also to explain to students what their expectations are, so do good school leaders use approaches similar to rubrics as a way of helping teachers understand what is expected of them. In fact, many school systems have adopted new evaluation systems that combine appraisal of past performance with formative advice about future development.

For example, the state of Georgia has implemented the Teacher Keys Effectiveness System (TKES) as a way of "building teacher effectiveness and ensuring consistency and comparability throughout the state" (Georgia Department of Education 2019). TKES is built on a growth model of evaluation rather than a traditional judgment and ranking model.

The instrument used in evaluations is designed to elicit meaningful feedback about teacher performance from administrators and help teachers know in what areas further progress is needed. It also encourages effective teachers to share their knowledge with others in the school so that collectively they can have a greater impact on all students.

It provides a clear rubric for evaluation, identifies specific indicators by which success can be measured, suggests sample performance indicators that help make the process less subjective, and recommends questions that school leaders can ask teachers in order to help them adopt mutually acceptable goals.

To get the full benefits of TKES, school leaders need to meet with their administrative team to discuss the best ways of interpreting how these state-wide standards are best applied to the distinctive needs of students at that particular school. They're encouraged to use multiple data sources (such as both formal and informal classroom observations, documentation of prac-tices, and sample student evidence that the teacher has met the criteria) as a way of obtaining as complete a picture of the teacher's effectiveness as possible.

Some administrators will choose to combine the evaluation process with ongoing mentoring by conducting a preconference during which the goals of the evaluation are explained, a scheduled observation during which informa-tion is collected, and a postconference during which meaningful feedback can be provided.

HELPING THE GOOD BECOME GREAT

As we've seen, a typical school environment is one in which the number of good teachers far exceeds the number of teachers whose performance is below expectations. As a result, school leaders have to approach the evalua-tion process aware that their largest task is not helping poor teachers become satisfactory but helping good teachers become great. That process can actual-ly be quite challenging.

First of all, when coaching a good teacher, it's very important to establish from the start that you're not giving the person advice because he or she did anything wrong. To the contrary, you're giving advice because you've seen the excellent work this teacher has done and you're aware that even greater achievement is possible.

As a result, any ideas you share about new approaches to consider or alternative methods should be regarded as a sign of how much confidence you have in that person. It's almost as though you're lending your "best tools" to someone you can trust to use them properly.

Second, identify what the good teacher does well and build on those strengths instead of focusing on where improvement may be possible and eliminating those weaknesses. In chapter 1, the concept of appreciative in-quiry was explored, and it was noted that school improvement plans work best when administrators identify what's already working, celebrate those strengths, and encourage more of those successful activities. A similar ap-proach works well when school leaders are trying to coach their good faculty members in the ways of becoming even better.

Dwelling on weaknesses often makes teachers defensive or causes them to distrust the administration's motives. Building on strengths helps the school to capitalize on the assets of its effective teachers and alerts them to the fact that their valuable contributions are being recognized.

The following three-step plan is often an effective way to help good teachers become great.

1. Identify some aspect of the teacher's performance that, while already of high quality, the teacher wishes to refine even further.
2. Discuss some possible benefits—such as an award, publication, promotion, or other recognition—that could occur if the teacher continues to make progress in the area of performance you've identified.
3. Work with the teacher to find some relatively easy first step (i.e., a task that could be completed within a week or two without considerable effort) that could start the teacher on the path toward attaining the benefits you outlined.

The benefits you identify in the second step are intended to get the teacher excited and motivated enough to want to embark on a personal improvement plan, and the easily attained goal you agree on in the third step will make sure that this process gets under way immediately.

In their book, *The Power of Moments* (2017), Chip and Dan Heath discuss why this approach to mentoring successful people works so well.

> Mentors push. [Those who are mentored] stretch. If you mentor someone—a student, an employee, a relative—you might wonder about the best way to give them a productive push. A good starting place is a two-part formula cited in a paper by the psychologist David Scott Yeager and eight colleagues: high standards + assurance. . . . *High standards + assurance* is a powerful formula, but ultimately it's just a statement of expectations. What great mentors do is add two more elements: direction and support. *I have high expectations for you and I know you can meet them. So try this new challenge and if you fail, I'll help you recover.* That's mentorship in two sentences. It sounds simple, yet it's powerful enough to transform careers. (Heath and Heath 2017, pp. 122–23)

The study they cite is Yeager, Purdie-Vaughns, Garcia, Apfel, Brzustoski, Master, Hessert, Williams, and Cohen, 2014. By coaching your good teachers in this way, you are providing the winning combination of setting high standards, expressing complete confidence that these standards will be met, offering direction on how to begin, and providing additional support, if needed.

USING EVALUATIONS TO IMPROVE PERFORMANCE

Of course, not everyone on our faculty will be a superstar. Even though, in a population that skews toward excellence, the evaluation process shouldn't be used primarily to identify poor performers, any evaluation method that combines review of past performance with the establishment of future goals has the ability to identify and assist those who are struggling. Those teachers who do not meet expectations during the formal review process can be offered remediation. Those whose performance problems are particularly severe or who do not improve after remediation can be terminated.

But in order for the evaluation process to have a meaningful effect on improvement, teachers who need help should be told precisely in which areas they are not meeting expectations, what they are doing that is ineffective, and what steps they can take to do better. If necessary, a formal plan of professional development can be drafted to make sure that teachers know exactly what needs to be done and how they can get the help they need.

Regular checkpoints throughout the year can be created for teachers to share and assess their progress. This process will allow administrators to become fully aware of all action steps planned at the departmental level.

School leaders can encourage teachers and department heads to work for continual improvement in their action plans by remembering that student learning must always be the highest goal, all plans should be grounded in the mission, vision, and values of the school, and just as students differ in their needs, so do teachers. Members of the faculty and staff can't create an environment dedicated to student growth if they don't also create an environment where their colleagues can grow and develop.

When providing advice on how members of the faculty and staff can improve, it's important to focus on the *behavior* that needs to be changed, not the *person* who is engaging in that behavior. People are entitled to their own personalities. They can be as ill-tempered, self-centered, or arrogant as they like. Only when those personality traits cause people to behave in ways that interfere with the school's mission should school leaders become involved. Even then, it's the person's actions, not his or her character, that should be the focus of the evaluation.

In general, evaluation aimed at improving poor performance should always begin with the following questions:

- What is the actual problem I'm observing? What tangible harm is being done?
- What are the specific actions or behaviors of the faculty member that are causing those problems? In other words, what behavior can I observe and document?

- What are the specific steps I need the faculty member to take in order to eliminate or reduce those problems? How will I know when a desired change has actually occurred?

Prepare very carefully for your oral evaluation sessions. You always want to know in advance what message you wish to convey and (even more importantly) what you'll *never* say to the person, even when provoked. During the evaluation, make it a genuine conversation. Find out the other person's perspective on issues. Encourage buy-in when setting goals or offering suggestions for improvement. Unless the person's performance is so bad that you are not renewing his or her contract, don't just talk about problems; celebrate strengths, too.

Take your time in oral evaluation sessions. Provide enough examples of each behavior that needs to be improved so that your overall message is clear. But take your time in offering praise as well. People need a chance to feel good about what they're doing right.

Never mix an evaluation session with any other sort of meeting. Doing so makes the evaluation seem less important. An evaluation session should always be a separate and somewhat formal conversation between a supervisor and the person who is being evaluated.

Be aware of the "subtext" of your meeting. If your facial expression doesn't match your words—if you seem to be taking severe problems too lightly or appear to be disapproving even when you're complimenting excellent performance—you undermine the message you're trying to convey. Even if your system does not require it, it's probably a good idea to follow any oral evaluation with a written summary of the issues discussed. In that way, there won't be any misunderstanding later of exactly what was discussed and which goals were set for the future.

There are similar principles to keep in mind when creating a written evaluation, including a memo of understanding after an oral evaluation. To begin with, a written evaluation should never be sent immediately after it's written. Read it over again a few days after you originally drafted it to make certain that it's as clear as you intended it. Ask yourself, if you were receiving such a document, what you would conclude about the author's overall *intention* and *tone*. Is that indeed what you'd hoped to convey?

Base your remarks only on established and consistent standards of performance. Remember what was stated earlier in this chapter: good teachers share their rubrics with students before they grade them so that the students know in advance what they're supposed to do. Good administrators do the same thing with the standards they'll use to evaluate the faculty and staff.

BECOMING PROACTIVE IN IMPROVING TEACHER PERFORMANCE

In order to avoid having to provide remediation to fix a problem, it is worth considering what resources school leaders can provide to teachers so that problems don't arise in the first place. In particular, new teachers often need help so that they'll be prepared to succeed. Their educational training may have grounded them in appropriate pedagogical strategies, but it is often unclear to a new member of the school community how best to excel *in this specific environment.*

Some of this preparation can be done during the onboarding process. Prior to the start of the year, all new teachers should be introduced to the procedures that may be unique to that particular school, such as how to take attendance, where to sign out supplies, how to make photocopies, and so on. Whenever possible, it's a good idea to pair a mentor with the new teacher to help review progress and discuss challenges *before* they emerge during a formal evaluation.

But orientation is not enough. Many high schools and colleges have re-placed old-fashioned one-week orientations of new students with first-year experiences, realizing that students can only absorb a limited amount of information in such a short period. The first-year experience extends the onboarding process over an entire year, introducing information only when it becomes relevant to the students and giving them time to absorb it. If this system works so well for students, why aren't academic leaders doing some-thing similar for members of the faculty and staff?

A faculty and staff first-year-experience program can avoid many of the problems that appear on evaluations by addressing performance issues and misunderstandings of policies before they become serious issues. School leaders should always remember that there's a shortage of qualified teachers in high-need areas, particularly at certain grade levels. Since there aren't long lines of great teachers waiting to get jobs, school leaders need to do a better job of helping the ones they have get better.

Supporting teachers through relevant professional development (related to topics that are specific to their work) goes a long way toward improving instruction. It has to be a priority for administrators to help teachers improve by setting aside sufficient time for peer observations and by providing teach-er coaches for those who need extra support.

Collaboration—teachers helping other teachers—is one of the most effec-tive processes schools can adopt to increase the level of learning among all students, regardless of their backgrounds or past performance. Collaboration also builds a sense of community within the faculty. School leaders can help to develop a stronger sense of community among the faculty by encouraging these collaborative efforts, recognizing the accomplishments of individual teachers, improving teacher appreciation activities with parent groups, and sponsoring faculty social functions.

People who work together don't develop a sense of community by knowing one another as colleagues. They develop it by knowing one another as three-dimensional human beings. Social functions play an important role in improving the quality of education at a school by creating bonds among teachers and staff members that result in a mutually supportive team.

CONCLUDING REMARKS

The best time to begin the evaluation process isn't when you notice the due date coming up on your calendar; it's the day after the last evaluation was concluded. If you keep notes about the performance of each teacher and staff member throughout the year, the process becomes easier for you and more productive for them. You're less likely to focus only on mistakes each person made because you'll have a more complete record of achievements to draw on. And if you do have to address weaknesses in performance, you'll have specific examples that you can cite when providing constructive advice on how that person can do better in the future.

A CASE STUDY IN FACULTY AND STAFF EVALUATION

A friend of yours has recently begun a position as head of school at Missed Opportunities Elementary School and needs your help. Since your friend has not had much experience with evaluating members of the faculty and staff, you're being asked to read over one of the written evaluations before it is sent.

"I'm having some trouble getting the phrasing exactly right for Frieda Gough, who teaches second grade," your friend tells you. "Frieda shows a lot of promise, and I'm afraid some other district is going to snap her up. She's really very creative in the classroom and attentive to all the individual needs of her students. The other teachers all consider Frieda a wonderful colleague, and, even though she's relatively new here at Missed Opportunities, she's already seen as having a great deal of leadership potential.

"I do need to bring one thing to her attention, though," your friend continues. "She seems a bit intimidated by the other, more experienced teachers, even though her ideas are often better than theirs are. I need her to speak up more at teacher meetings and, frankly, just to have a lot more confidence. But I'm not quite sure how to say that. Could you look at what I've written in her annual evaluation and give me some suggestions? I was on the verge of sending her the letter as it's written here, but then I remembered how good you are when it comes to faculty and staff evaluation."

Your friend gives you the written evaluation, which is reproduced below.

Annual Evaluation: Ms. Frieda Gough, Second Grade

Over the next year, you are instructed to become more vocal at teacher meetings and to express your opinions more openly. Despite any criticism that may arise from other, more experienced teachers, it is imperative for the attainment of our pedagogical goals that your perspectives and views be shared with your colleagues.

When teachers fail at Missed Opportunities Elementary School, it is more often because they are too hesitant to share good ideas than because they are too vocal in sharing bad ones. Your success in our school is dependent on your willingness to exercise the leadership potential others believe you to have.

In addition, your classroom teaching appears to be quite creative, and it has been reported that you are attentive to the individual needs of all your students. Your colleagues like working with you.

Overall Evaluation: Exceeds Expectations

What advice do you give your friend after reading this evaluation?

DISCUSSION OF THE CASE STUDY

Your friend's written evaluation is not likely to have the effect that he or she intended. Although, when speaking to you, most of the observations were about the strengths of Frieda Gough and what a loss her departure would be for the school, the evaluation devotes more than half of the text addressing a relatively minor criticism and very little text recognizing Frieda's obvious strengths.

In addition, the tone of the evaluation seems unnecessarily negative. Frieda is "instructed" to improve. This change is "imperative." Frieda is informed about the circumstances under which "teachers fail." As a result, the impression the recipient of this letter might have is that the person who is being evaluated is performing poorly. Only at the very end of the letter are any positive achievements mentioned, followed by the conclusion that Frieda has exceeded expectations (a result that may actually come as a surprise in light of how negative the earlier remarks have been).

You might recommend that your friend rewrite the letter entirely, devoting far more text to Frieda's accomplishments and celebrating her successes. The recommendation that she become more vocal in meetings may best be omitted from the letter entirely. It is more the advice that a mentor might give someone privately than a serious criticism that deserves to be addressed in an annual evaluation.

If the goal is indeed to dissuade Frieda Gough from "being snapped up" by other school districts, the current version of the letter is unlikely to achieve that goal. It would be better to rewrite the letter with a more positive and constructive tone, one that is far more appropriate for a faculty member who has the potential to become a rising star.

KEY POINTS IN THIS CHAPTER

- Although faculty and staff evaluation remains a very common method for trying to improve performance, it isn't particularly effective.
- The faculty and staff of a school do not constitute a random distribution, so any evaluation system that seeks to force results into a "bell-shaped curve" is likely to distort the data.
- Faculty and staff evaluation can be diagnostic, formative, summative, and summative-formative. If schools use evaluation only for summative purposes, they diminish its value even further.
- Evaluation should be future oriented and include goal setting rather than merely retrospective or focused on areas of weakness.
- Helping good performers become great adds a dimension of coaching or mentoring to the evaluation process. Those being evaluated should be given an exciting, long-term goal to motivate them and an easy, short-term goal to ensure that progress will begin quickly.
- When performance does need to be improved, the evaluator should focus on the behavior that needs to change, not the personality or character of the person who needs to change it.
- Effective onboarding processes, such as first-year-experience programs for the faculty and staff, can help avoid problems before they even arise.
- Performance often improves most significantly because of cooperative and collaborative interaction with peers, not instructions from supervisors.

REFERENCES

Georgia Department of Education. 2019. "Teacher Keys Effectiveness System." http://www.gadoe.org/School-Improvement/Teacher-and-Leader-Effectiveness/Pages/Teacher-Keys-Effectiveness-System.aspx

Heath, D., & Heath, C. (2019). *The Power of Moments*. New York, NY: Random House.

Jacobs, C. S. 2009. *Management Rewired: Why Feedback Doesn't Work and Other Surprising Lessons from the Latest Brain Science*. New York, NY: Portfolio.

Jacobs, C. S. 2010. "Tis the Season for Reviews. Bah, Humbug!" *Psychology Today*. https://www.psychologytoday.com/us/blog/management-rewired/201011/tis-the-season-reviews-bah-humbug-0

Nickols, F. 2007. "Performance Appraisal: Weighed and Found Wanting in the Balance." *Journal for Quality & Participation 30*(1): 13–16.

Yeager, D. S., V. Purdie-Vaughns, J. Garcia, N. Apfel, P. Brzustoski, A. Master, W. T. Hessert, M. E. Williams, and G. L. Cohen. 2014. "Breaking the Cycle of Mistrust: Wise Interventions to Provide Critical Feedback Across the Racial Divide." *Journal of Experimental Psychology: General 143*(2): 804–24.

RESOURCES

Barker, C. L., and C. J. Searchwell. 2010. *Writing Meaningful Teacher Evaluations—Right Now!!: The Principal's Quick-Start Reference Guide* (3rd ed.). Thousand Oaks, CA: Corwin.

Buller, J. L. 2013. *Best Practices in Faculty Evaluation*. San Francisco, CA: Jossey-Bass.

Danielson, C., and T. L. McGreal. 2000. *Teacher Evaluation to Enhance Professional Practice.* Alexandria, VA: Association for Supervision and Curriculum Development.

Darling-Hammond, L. 2013. *Getting Teacher Evaluation Right: What Really Matters for Effectiveness and Improvement.* New York, NY: Teachers College Press.

Marshall, K. 2013. *Rethinking Teacher Supervision and Evaluation: How to Work Smart, Build Collaboration, and Close the Achievement Gap* (2nd ed.). San Francisco, CA: Jossey-Bass.

Marzano, R. J., and M. Toth. 2013. *Teacher Evaluation That Makes a Difference: A New Model for Teacher Growth and Student Achievement.* Alexandria, VA: Association for Supervision and Curriculum Development.

Chapter Five

Student Academic Challenges

If you ask members of the public about the best way to help students overcome their academic challenges, many people will tell you that schools just need to "get back to the way they used to be." They'll talk about the successes of the one-room schoolhouse where there weren't any behavioral issues to distract students, teacher-led prayer set a tone of morality that guided students to make constructive choices, and mass shootings were unheard of. In this halcyon period, older students willingly mentored their younger peers, parents never got divorced, and mothers stayed at home, taking care of their children and preparing three hot meals a day.

Like so many memories of an ideal past, however, that recollection of a once perfect school environment is a myth. As Jonathan Zimmerman points out in *Small Wonder: The Little Red Schoolhouse in History and Memory* (2009), the school of the past was likely to have been overcrowded, underfunded, and staffed by teachers who were only slightly better educated than the students they taught. The "little red schoolhouse" was rarely even red, since paint was expensive and public schools outside of areas inhabited by the wealthy had very little funding for even routine maintenance.

Undeniably, students today face academic challenges that students of previous generations encountered far less often. They deal with learning disabilities, not because those disabilities didn't exist in the past but because they went undiagnosed. Students who couldn't read or perform calculations as rapidly as others were dismissed as lazy or just plain stupid. Students today deal more regularly with psychological challenges—sometimes their own, sometimes those of their classmates—not because those challenges didn't exist in the past but because the children who had them were unlikely to be allowed in school in the first place.

Our digital society exposes students at a very young age to violence, hatred, and intolerance that their parents and grandparents may have encountered only later in life, but it also permits them to travel virtually to distant lands and galaxies, peer inside atoms, and receive instruction that can be uniquely tailored to their individual needs.

If academic leaders are to address the academic challenges of students now and in the future, they're unlikely to find much guidance in romanticized images of the past. Fortunately, however, tools exist that can help teachers and administrators deliver the type of academic support that students deserve, and those tools are to be found all around us in the modern world.

Neuroscience has revealed much that was previously not known about how students learn and why some students seem to learn more readily than others. Entrepreneurism has enticed venture capitalists to invest in bold initiatives to educate students in new ways. While many of those initiatives have failed, others have succeeded, in some cases spectacularly, and provided lessons about what might work in the school of tomorrow. And social networking makes it possible to expose administrators, teachers, and students to best practices, not just in their own districts, but anywhere in the world.

What have neuroscience, entrepreneurism, and social networking taught us about what works most effectively in meeting students' academic challenges?

METACOGNITION

Metacognition, the awareness and understanding of one's own thought processes, has in many ways been part of an educator's toolkit for decades, perhaps centuries. Math teachers have long insisted that students not only find the correct answer but also "show their work" so that the steps they used to reach their conclusions can be analyzed. And as early as 1890, the psychologist and philosopher William James (1842–1910) used the term *introspection* in his *Principles of Psychology* to describe a phenomenon that most people would now regard as metacognition.

In modern educational theory, however, the (re-)introduction of metacognition as a major learning strategy is usually credited to the developmental psychologist John Flavell, who, in 1976, used the term in a chapter on problem-solving that he contributed to Lauren Resnick's *The Nature of Intelligence* (1976). The fundamental idea behind metacognition is that students should be regularly asked to explain the *why* behind their answers, not merely the *what*.

This process becomes particularly important in middle school and later since research conducted by Marcel Veenman and others at the University of Leiden indicates that children start developing skills at metacognition and self-reflection at about age twelve and that this ability continues to expand as young adults enter their early twenties. (See, for example, Veenman and Desoete, 2006.) By encouraging students to become increasingly proficient at metacognition, teachers help students not only learn but also learn how to learn, thus reinforcing habits that will continue to be beneficial throughout the students' lives.

Back in the period of "the little red schoolhouse," it was assumed that all students could learn in the same way. The teacher lectured and perhaps illustrated a few examples, and then students were expected to imitate the technique and make it their own. Those who couldn't do so were regarded as dense, incapable, or lazy and sometimes assigned to a "slow group" for learning so that they wouldn't impede the progress of the "bright" students (i.e., the students who tended to learn in the way that the teacher had learned).

For example, when learning to spell words, teachers or parents would write out the correct spelling of a word and give it to the students to memorize. If the child was dyslexic or had some other undiagnosed learning challenge, he or she would spell the word incorrectly on the test, be marked wrong, and develop a self-identity as a "poor speller" or "stupid person." That student would thus be unlikely to approach the next set of vocabulary words with much confidence.

It rarely occurred to teachers to try to help the student learn how to spell through other techniques than memorization, such as creating a spelling hopscotch board on which students could repeat spellings as they played the game or preparing a word-search puzzle containing the spelling words for that unit.

In the 1970s, the traditional approach of "teaching by telling" began to be challenged as researchers like David Kolb, Peter Honey, Alan Mumford, Walter Burke Barbe, Neil Fleming, and others found that different students had different "styles" of learning. (See, for example, Kolb 2015; Mumford 1997; Barbe, Swassing, and Milone, 1979). Eventually, as a result of these studies, many teachers came to assume that each student had one of three dominant learning styles: *auditory* (the student learned best through listening to lectures), *visual* (the student learned best through looking at illustrations or diagrams), and *kinesthetic* or *experiential.*

More recent research has, however, challenged this paradigm and demonstrated that, regardless of how students scored on "learning style inventories," the vast majority of them learned best through a combination of *seeing* and *doing* (Marzano 1998; Constantinidou and Baker 2002). Most damning of all, an exhaustive study conducted in 2008 by the Association for Psychological Sciences concluded that "at present, there is no adequate evidence base to justify incorporating learning styles assessments into general educational practice" (Pashler, McDaniel, Rohrer, and Bjork 2008).

The result is that, while students may feel more *comfortable* with certain learning modalities, there is little tangible evidence that they have innate or inalterable "learning styles." The tendency, therefore, is for scholars in the field of education and developmental psychology to no longer refer to *learning styles* but instead to refer to a student's *learning preferences*.

Even so, metacognitive practices can help students understand their current learning preferences and at times develop greater comfort and proficiency with other modalities of learning. They may also learn that, simply because they are more introverted than other students, that doesn't mean that they are rude or shy; they simply process information and recover their mental energy more efficiently in private (as opposed to extraverts who prefer to think aloud and recover their mental energy more efficiently in groups).

Metacognitive activities can begin as simply as asking, "Why did you answer that way?" or, "What was the first thing you did when you began solving this problem/answering this question?" As metacognitive skills develop, these questions can become more complex, incorporating such processes as

- *Intentionality*: "What do you already know about this topic?" "What assumptions are you making about the activity we'll be doing next?" "What have we studied before that could help you in our next unit?" "What do you believe you'll be able to do when we complete this unit that you can't do now?"
- *The muddiest point*: "What about the material that we explored today/in this unit/in this term do you still find most confusing?" "If there was one aspect of this topic that you wished you understood better, what would it be?" "What questions still need to be answered so that we understand this concept completely?"
- *Reflection*: "What did you think this concept meant before we began this activity?" "What do you think it means now?" "What was the most important insight you had during this discussion?" "What aspect of the exercise did you find most challenging? How did you overcome that challenge?" "What should you do differently next time you are dealing with a question/problem/issue like this one?"

At the high school level, metacognitive journals are valuable ways for students to explore questions like these in their own way and at their own pace. At any grade level, assignments that include essays of appropriate length and complexity develop metacognition much more rapidly than do multiple-choice exams, matching exercises, and true-false quizzes.

The latter types of activities may be easier and more objective for teachers to grade, but they are far less effective in helping students overcome their academic challenges. Essays help teachers produce the sort of *word-rich* classroom environment that provides students with the vocabulary they need to examine their own thought processes, monitor their own learning, and develop strategies for their own continued progress.

In more advanced classes, metacognition can be developed by repeatedly asking students questions like the following:

- What do you believe is important to understand and learn in [THIS SUB-JECT OR UNIT]?
- What do you believe to be essential characteristics of successful students in [THIS SUBJECT OR UNIT]?
- How will you study and prepare for exams in [THIS SUBJECT OR UNIT]?

Students can also be taught to take notes in the structured manner known as the *transfer journal*. With a transfer journal, rather than simply writing down what a teacher says or copying words from a marker board or PowerPoint presentation, students define and interpret new concepts according to the following structure:

- Idea: How would you define this concept in your own words (not necessarily the words used by the teacher)?
- Interpretation: Why do you think this concept is important enough for us to devote class time to it?
- Connection: How does this concept relate to other ideas discussed in this class or other courses that you've taken?
- Transfer: How would you apply this concept to a practical example?
- Insight (optional): Did you have any "Aha! moments" as you learned this concept? If so, what were they?

The principle of the transfer journal is that it teaches students how to learn by not merely engaging in rote memorization but by relating each new concept to what they already understand. For more information on how metacognition can be used in the classroom, see Saundra Yancy McGuire and Stephanie McGuire's *Teach Students How to Learn* (2016).

UNDERSTANDING MOTIVATION

The authors of this book conducted a focus group session with forty-seven active teachers at various types of schools—public and private, elementary and secondary—and asked them a number of questions, including, "What are the top three academic challenges you feel your students face?" One of the most frequent responses had to do with lack of motivation. The following are just a few examples of what teachers cited as the causes of student academic challenges:

- "The top three academic challenges students face are lack of motivation, difficulty managing time, and being confident in their skillset."
- "Equity in educational experience (resources, instruction, family/socioeconomic issues); lack of engagement/motivation; lack of opportunities to problem solve/apply learning in real world situations."
- "Motivation, focus, engagement with subjects uninteresting to them."
- "Absence of motivation. In high schools there are other priorities in life (this can be as obvious as friends, or it can be something students don't want to share like poverty and even homelessness). Stress and pressure of standardized tests: These tests are not written to identify what a student knows and are not representative of students with learning disabilities. Lack of study skills: in elementary grades, students are handed information or are not made to think for themselves. When coming to high school, it is difficult to then teach these skills when there is no foundation."
- "I teach freshmen boys at an all-male Catholic school. The biggest challenges are motivation, lack of basic skills to help them understand content, and time management. We *are* a private school, yet I find these challenges from students who are coming in from both public and private schools. Overall, many of them are just simply not prepared for high school."
- "Lack of motivation, lack of basic skills, lack of self-discipline."

Those responses should be surprising to no one who has spent any time in a contemporary classroom. And yet, this frequent reference to a general lack of motivation on the part of today's students leads to an interesting question: *Why do so many students find it difficult to become motivated to master a skill or concept that will improve their lives but are motivated enough to spend hours mastering a video game or a sport that often requires substantially more concentration and effort?* In order to answer this question, it's first necessary to understand what psychology and neuroscience have taught us about impulse control and childhood development.

By the time most people are adults, they're familiar with the concept of delayed gratification, the notion that it is often beneficial to defer an immediate reward for a larger reward in the future. But many children have not yet developed the capacity to postpone satisfying a current desire in the hopes of achieving a more significant goal in the future.

In Walter Mischel's famous Marshmallow Experiment at Stanford University, children were left alone in a room with a marshmallow for fifteen minutes. They were told that, if they could resist eating the marshmallow until the researcher returned, they would be given two marshmallows at that time (Mischel 2015). Mischel discovered that only about a third of the children were able to defer gratification long enough to receive the second marshmallow. But the most amazing results that emerged came from a follow-up, longitudinal study. Children who had demonstrated an early ability to defer gratification turned out later in life to have higher scores in the aggregate on standardized tests (Shoda, Mischel, and Peake 1990) and greater activity in the prefrontal cortex when they were confronted with similar challenges dealing with delayed gratification (Casey, Somerville, Gotlib, Ayduk, Franklin, Askren, Jonides, Berman, Wilson, Teslovich, Glover, Zayas, Mischel, and Shoda, 2011). In other words, children who had developed an ability to resist temptation early in their lives continued to demonstrate certain types of intellectual advantages throughout their lives.

Many teachers' initial response to these studies might be either to redouble their efforts to teach children impulse control early in their lives or to assume that students with an innate ability to defer gratification will succeed while other students will struggle. But if the goal is to help students overcome their academic challenges, neither of these conclusions seems acceptable. It's not appropriate to dismiss two-thirds of a class as all but destined to struggle, and trying to inculcate habits that a student's cerebral and emotional development isn't yet ready for isn't likely to be effective.

These observations bring us back to the question raised earlier: Why do students often find it difficult to spend thirty minutes learning vocabulary or solving math problems but pleasant to spend hour after hour mastering a video game or sports? The answer to this question, as we now know, is that students, like everyone else, do have motivation. It's merely that schools today don't often tap into that motivation as effectively as do video game designers and coaches.

Consider for a moment the difference between a child's experience with a videogame and his or her experience in school.

- Progress: In a video game, the player *levels up* whenever certain goals have been achieved. Early on in the game, leveling up is very easy and occurs quite often; as the player's skill develops, leveling up becomes more challenging and occurs more rarely. In school, students "level up" once a year from one grade level to the next, all at the same time, and, in the majority of cases, almost automatically, regardless of achievement. (Adults will understand the motivation that leveling up provides if they've ever worked harder to attain the goal of "10,000 steps per day" on their electronic fitness trainers or taken an additional flight to achieve gold, platinum, or diamond levels in a frequent-flyer program.)
- Narrative: In a video game, players are involved in an adventure, such as a quest, a mystery, or a battle. In school, students often aren't aware of the value that the skills they're learning will eventually have, leading to such

questions as, "Will I ever use this?" and "Will this be on the test?" In the case of the latter question, for example, the implied narrative of school is merely to pass (or to receive an A on) the next test and then to move on to the test after that.

- Personal best: In a video game, players may be competing against others, but they are also competing against their own previous scores through strategies such as collecting experience points, the discovery of new tasks when certain goals have been completed, and the listing of scores on leaderboards. In school, students measure their personal best by grades and scores that may imply false equivalents. For example, a student who receives a 96 in math but an 88 in Spanish may conclude, "I'm good at math but bad at learning languages," even though those two scores may have been calculated very differently.

- Social facilitation: In a video game (and in athletics), players may be motivated to try harder and improve their skills because they're part of a mutually supportive team. In school, teachers usually encourage students to "do your own work," "keep your eyes on your own paper," and thus imply that independent success is the only type of success that matters.

- Immersion: In a video game (and in athletics), players are actively engaged at all times and are stimulated auditorily, visually, and experientially all at the same time. Video games and sports are totally immersive experiences. In school, much of a student's experience may be passive, listening to a teacher explain a concept or other students recite and work out problems.

As a result of these differences, some researchers have argued that schools should engage in *gamification*, the application of insights gained from sports and video games to pedagogical methods (McGonigal 2011; 2016). The authors, however, believe that gamification is only part of a larger phenomenon. What school leaders need to understand is that students' motivation to overcome challenges increases through a specific type of social interaction and experiential activity.

In a study conducted by Jal Mehta of the Harvard Graduate School in Education and Sarah Fine of San Diego's High Tech High Graduate School of Education (Mehta and Fine 2019), students were found to respond very differently to traditional academic classes—including courses widely believed to be innovative in design, honors, and advanced placement courses—and to cocurricular activities like debate clubs and play productions or extracurricular activities like sports teams and nonacademic clubs.

> In essence, two different logics reign in the same buildings. Before the final bell, we treat students as passive recipients of knowledge whose interests and identities matter little. After the final bell—in newspaper, debate, theater, ath-

letics and more—we treat students as people who learn by doing, people who can teach as well as learn, and people whose passions and ideas are worth cultivating. It should come as no surprise that when we asked students to reflect on their high school experiences, it was most often experiences like theater and debate that they cited as having influenced them in profound ways. The truly powerful core classes that we found—and at every school there were some—echoed what we saw in extracurriculars. Rather than touring students through the textbook, teachers invited students to participate in the authentic work of the field. (Mehta and Fine 2019, 4)

Most classes, even those taught by star teachers, tended to be lacking in experiential opportunities and to discourage social interaction. By contrast, cocurricular and extracurricular activities tended to engage students specifically because they immersed the students in whatever they were doing and encouraged them to learn from one another, not merely a designated teacher or coach.

What Mehta and Fine (2019) recommended, therefore, was that if schools were truly interested in overcoming student academic challenges, they should do the following:

- Include more actual experiments in which students make genuine discoveries rather than merely repeat "experiments" in which the probable outcome is already known.
- Reward actual learning and mastery of concepts rather than "seat time" or time-on-task.
- Provide a greater sense of context for what is learned. Students are less likely to ask "Why do I need to know this?" and more likely to make rapid progress if they understand that the theories, processes, and concepts they learn are applicable to real-world problems.
- Deemphasize traditional academic boundaries, and incorporate more problem-based learning strategies. Solving such problems as, "How do I budget effectively so that my income more than covers my expenses?" "What are possible techniques that could be used to reduce poverty and improve public health?" or "How do people interact effectively with cultures very different from their own?" still require students to employ the scientific method, become mathematically literate, comprehend and communicate in other languages, and develop the skills commonly associated with pre-K–12 education, but it does so in a way that makes those traditional disciplines immediately meaningful.

There is also one other major difference between the experience most students have in their classes and in their cocurricular and extracurricular activities. While preparing a play, students develop intensely close relationships with the director. While participating on an athletic team, students develop intensely close relationships with the coach. While performing in a band or orchestra, students develop intensely close relationships with the conductor.

Those relationships are all but impossible (except for perhaps a handful of students) in most current classrooms, which are too large, too exam focused, and too regimented for teachers to mentor everyone in their charge. In short, the very strategies adopted to improve the quality of education—frequent standardized tests performed in large impersonal classes—have actually furthered its decline. They may allow legislators and administrators to offer quantified "evidence" of improvement, but they do little to cause students to become engaged, lifelong learners with an intrinsic motivation to conduct lives well led.

FALLING FORWARD

Perhaps the most insidious effect of standardized testing on students is the implication that the vast majority of questions have one and only one right answer and that, if they don't provide that answer, they are "wrong" and have somehow "failed." That common impression is often justified with the response, "But that's how it is in 'the real world,' and the sooner students come to understand that no one becomes a winner simply by participating, the better."

The fact of the matter is, however, that in many of the most important experiences students will have once they leave school there may be numerous correct answers (or no correct answers at all), and those who don't hit upon the "one correct answer" haven't failed.

A scientist in a lab doesn't expect to validate or disprove a hypothesis with a single experiment. Experiments that don't work out aren't "failures"; they're clues about new directions to pursue.

A business professional who is marketing a product doesn't give up because research indicates that potential customers don't like the approach taken in a proposed advertisement. This information is used to plan a new marketing strategy and then, if the new strategy also doesn't work, subsequent strategies after that.

An entrepreneur whose first endeavor doesn't work out hasn't "failed"; he or she has gained important insights into how to succeed at some future endeavor.

A pianist whose first attempt to master a sonata doesn't give up and avoid trying again because he or she has "failed." The pianist keeps practicing so that his or her performance improves.

A witticism commonly attributed to Albert Einstein, but actually first recorded in this form by the mystery novelist Rita Mae Brown, holds that, "Insanity is doing the same thing over and over again, but expecting different results" (Brown 1983, 68). In May 2019, the cartoonist Jef Mallett issued a rejoinder in his syndicated strip *Frazz*: "If doing the same thing over and over and expecting different results is the definition of insanity, what's the definition of practice?" This response indicates something significant about how genuine learning often occurs in "the real world": it comes at the end of a series of, sometimes very long and painful, "failures."

The concept involved in this learning process is known as *falling forward* (or *failing forward*), a concept made popular by the leadership guru John C. Maxwell, who provides the following advice on how best to learn, grow, and eventually succeed: "Fail early, fail often, but always fail forward. Turn your mistakes into stepping-stones for success" (Maxwell 2007, pp. 203).

The idea of falling forward is to see the inevitable setbacks and disappointments that come our way, not as impenetrable barriers to success, but as inspirations for continued progress. That strategy is well known to coaches, conductors, directors, and the other mentors involved in the immersion activities mentioned earlier, but is discouraged by the "teach to the test" mentality that regards success solely in terms of hitting certain targets, such as minimum scores on standardized tests, admission to prestigious colleges and universities, and earning an income that places the recipient in the top 1 percent of citizens.

A pedagogy based on helping students to fall forward would be more inquiry based and less driven by the rubrics developed for standardized tests. It would include more opportunities for students to learn about concepts by applying them rather than hearing about them. Here are some examples:

- Fewer experiments in science classes would simply re-create experiments first performed decades ago, and more experiments would involve actual discovery. For example, one exercise developed by the University of Texas at Austin has high school students (of any level) adopt research techniques to identify random collections of unknown organisms rather than merely learn about microorganisms from a textbook or presentation (Feng, Hawkins, Park, and Joseph, n.d.).
- Students would study plays by acting in them and then critiquing them, not merely reading about them in books.
- Mathematical concepts would be taught as part of community service projects where actual problems, not merely story problems, are solved.
- To whatever extent is possible, historical incidents would be studied by visiting the actual sites where they occurred (if not in person, then virtually), not by learning dates and reading dry summaries.
- Critical thinking, source analysis, and logical argumentation would be taught by having students engaged in formal, structured debates where evidence and reasoning would be valued over opinion and intensity of conviction.

These pedagogical strategies encourage students to *fall forward*. They won't make a new discovery, perform a play perfectly, communicate effectively with representatives of a different culture, solve complex problems, and engage in any other kind of immersion activity perfectly the first time. But they'll learn that practice makes perfect and that not getting "the answer" on a first attempt isn't a failure; it's a step in an ongoing process.

The authors aren't suggesting that problem-based, immersive learning replace traditional classroom practices entirely. Such a goal is neither practical nor, in the long term, desirable. There will always be concepts and techniques that must be demonstrated or explained before they can be applied in the field. But by increasing the number of inquiry-based activities in their classrooms, teachers create an environment that students are far more likely to find engaging and help them continue the process of developing into lifelong learners.

EDUCATING HOLISTICALLY

Immersive education is one way in which schools can educate students holistically by making the distinction between "life in school" and "life at home or in the community" less sharp. But there's another way that holistic education can help students overcome their academic challenges: by making it part of the school's mission to educate not just the students who attend classes but also the parents who send those students to classes and even the community at large.

Some of the most important insights gained in this area have come from the experiments conducted by entrepreneurs who are seeking to design a radically improved version of American education. The results of these experiments have, to put it bluntly, been mixed. There is a tendency for people to think either, "I'm successful, and what worked for me should work for everyone," or "Students would learn so much better if only the things I hated about going to school were eliminated."

Like charter schools, some experimental programs initiated by wealthy private investors have been highly successful. Many others, however, have not lived up to the expectations their founders had for them.

One experimental school with a particularly strong track record is the I Promise School in Akron, Ohio, funded in part by basketball legend LeBron James. The vast majority of this school's "$2 million budget is funded by the district, roughly the same amount per pupil that it spends in other schools" (Green 2019). Many of the immersive and holistic innovations found in the I Promise School are familiar from elementary and high schools elsewhere and adhere to the best practices outlined in this book. For example, students are greeted individually by staff members as they arrive, and efforts are made to make the learning experience engaging and exciting.

But it's the aspect of the school that's specifically funded by James's foundation that appears to be having the greatest impact.

> The school is unusual in the resources and attention it devotes to parents, which educators consider a key to its success. Mr. James's foundation covers the cost of all expenses in the school's family resource center, which provides parents with G.E.D. preparation, work advice, health and legal services, and even a quarterly barbershop. The school negotiated with the Akron Education Association for an extra hour a day and an extended year to put into place programs intended to address students' social and emotional needs. (Green 2019)

One major academic challenge many students face isn't a function of their own abilities or levels of preparation; it's the environment they return to when the school day is done. When students return home to a word-rich environment that sets high standards for individual academic achievement, they're far more likely to succeed than are those students who return to families where the level of educational attainment has been low and the commitment to the importance of education even lower.

It's difficult to succeed academically when your parent is illiterate or only semiliterate, unemployed, relocated frequently, in prison, ill, or convinced that institutions exist to oppress, not to liberate, free minds. By including parents in its educational mission, the I Promise School sends a strong message that academic success is important, and it validates this message by providing the resources parents need to advance their own educations, hold down a well-paying job, and live a healthy lifestyle.

In a famous study first begun during the early 1960s, the High/Scope Perry Preschool Study in Ypsalanti, Michigan, a longitudinal comparison was made of two groups of African American children from low-income families. Fifty-eight children attended a high-quality preschool program, and sixty-five did not. Initially, the study was believed to be a failure, because there was little to no difference in academic performance between the two groups during the students' early years in elementary school.

But when the students were tracked over the course of the next forty years, it was discovered that, compared to the control group, the students who participated in the preschool program had

- a significantly higher likelihood of graduating from high school (most dramatically if they were female), higher literacy scores later in life, better relationships with their own children, higher rates of employment, and more stable living relationships; and

- lower reliance on social services, fewer lifetime arrests, and lower rates of conviction for violent crimes.

One of the conclusions of the study was that the preschool program was particularly effective in the long term because of its impact, not just on the participants themselves, but also on their families and living situations (Schweinhart, Montie, Xiang, Barnett, Belfield, and Nores, 2005).

The type of outreach provided by the I Promise School and the High/Scope Perry Preschool Study isn't financially possible for many other schools, including those that have barely enough resources to meet the basic needs of the children who are enrolled there. But it does highlight the fallacy of thinking that student educational challenges can be overcome simply through "one focus solutions," like providing more tutors, lengthening the class day or year, investing in technology, or pursuing any of the other solutions that districts and entrepreneurs alike have explored with mixed results.

A combination of all those strategies may be required, along with reductions in class size, diminishing the emphasis on standardized tests, providing more experiential and immersive education, and including parents as primary stakeholders in the school's pedagogical efforts.

CONCLUDING REMARKS

There will always be something attractive about quick-fix solutions to challenges in student academic achievement. "If we would only extend the school year," some say, while others argue that a return to phonics or daily prayer is the solution all students need.

The truth is that, just as no two students are alike, so it is with the strategies that school leaders must explore to improve student performance. Depending on your school's mission, the needs of the students it serves, and the expertise of your teachers, the path to greater academic achievement for your students is likely to be very different from that of schools even in your own area.

The authors of this book recommend increasing the number of metacognitive activities included in courses, helping teachers understand better how to tie their goals to the types of motivation that students actually have, making courses more immersive and experiential, teaching students to "fall forward" rather than to regard failure as a personal indictment, and thinking of the school's education mission more holistically are among the best ways to confront today's issues.

But these are ingredients, not a recipe. How you blend them into a method for moving forward requires insight into the distinctive challenges of your students and may well even vary significantly for different students in the school.

A CASE STUDY IN STUDENT ACADEMIC CHALLENGES

Imagine that you're a fourth-grade teacher, one of whose new students is Ellie Mentrie. As you're going through Ellie's records, you find that her third-grade teacher wrote the following learning profile, detailing what he observed regarding Ellie's interests and areas of motivation during the previous year.

Ellie Mentrie is a third-grade student who has demonstrated a number of special interests in school. Her *primary interest appears to be in technology*, as she has demonstrated that she enjoys activities that involve technology and computers, multimedia equipment, and communication.

Ellie's *second area of interest appears to be in athletics*. She is highly engaged whenever there are opportunities for physical activity and may be interested in learning about sports, nutrition, physical therapy, or sports medicine.

Ellie's *third area of interest appears to be in mathematics*. She works quickly and successfully with numbers, problems, patterns, and logic and also appears to enjoy using computers and working on logic puzzles and word problems.

Ellie also has demonstrated a preference for specific instructional styles. Her *preferred instructional style is through technology* that helps her learn by using various interactive multimedia devices and Internet content. Her *second choice of learning style is working in groups*, as she enjoys working together with other students in or out of class. Ellie *also enjoys programmed instruction* that may occur when she reads a chapter and then answers questions, or when she is asked to complete workbook pages after a review of some material in class.

Ellie also has a preferred product style. That is to say, there are certain kinds of products or assignments that Ellie likes to complete. Her *first product choice is artwork*, as she likes to draw, paint, or sculpt and may also enjoy choosing colors and working with design or texture. Her *second choice of product style is commercial*, as she has said on a number of occasions that she would like to start her own small business or sell a product. Ellie's *third choice of product style is audio-visual/display*. She enjoys organizing attractive arrangements of objects and will devote many hours to work where she can put information on boards or posters. She also may enjoy organizing materials and designing diagrams to visually display information.

As Ellie has a chance to consider some of her choices and think about what she really enjoys doing, it is our hope that these opportunities will enable her to fully develop her interests through the variety of exploratory activities in the Renzulli Learning System® database. When she takes a virtual field trip to a museum, interviews a favorite author on the web, or explores a historical site online, she will be learning to further explore her interests and learning styles.

These kinds of exploratory activities can introduce Ellie to new ideas and experiences and let her explore many possible interests.

How might you use this information to develop an individualized study plan that will provide Ellie with the best opportunity to succeed during the coming year?

DISCUSSION OF THE CASE STUDY

As you read the case study above, certain expressions should have leapt off the page for you: technology, athletics, mathematics, group work, art, commercial, and audio-visual. Like many students in the fourth grade, Ellie has not yet been pigeonholed (or pigeonholed herself) into being a "science student," "language arts student," "creative student," and so on. Your first task as a teacher might thus be to determine a way in which you can help Ellie build on her interests in all these areas without unnecessarily limiting her focus.

At the same time, this stage in Ellie's academic development is a good time to build on her skills in such areas as critical and creative thinking. For this reason, she may benefit from activities like the following:

- Imagine a type of business that would serve athletes, artists, or both. How would success be measured in such a business? How would mathematical procedures be used to track that success? What roles could other students play in a group project of this sort?
- Develop a video game or other computer application for use in business, athletics, or the creative world. Within the limits of a fourth-grader's ability to code, what logical systems and flow of information would be necessary for the game or software? Do other students in the class have areas of strength or interests that complement Ellie's and that can be incorporated into this project?
- Create a system for tracking the nutritional needs and training activities of athletes, dancers, and others. What information would need to be recorded, and what mathematical processes would be necessary to demonstrate and encourage progress? How can the results be displayed in an informative and visually pleasing format?

Naturally, over the course of the year as you begin to know Ellie more as an individual, you'll probably develop even more creative activities that can engage Ellie at a high level and help her grow in her academic pursuits. But the suggestions above, as well as others that you thought of as you read the case study, may well be a good place to begin.

KEY POINTS IN THIS CHAPTER

- Neuroscience, entrepreneurism, and social networking have provided us with important insights into what works most effectively in meeting students' academic challenges.
- One of the most valuable pedagogical strategies teachers have is metacognition, the practice of guiding students to understand and become aware of their own thought processes.
- What were once regarded as learning *styles* are now more properly regarded as learning *preferences.*
- Preadult students are more likely to be motivated to succeed at tasks that include opportunities for social interaction, immersion, and experiential activities.
- A major obstacle to student academic progress is the inability many students have to "fall forward," regarding their mistakes as growth opportunities, not indications of personal failure.
- Educating holistically means not only providing a learning environment that engages "the entire student" but also, to whatever extent possible, educating parents and providing opportunities for students to learn within a structure that provides them with security and stability.

REFERENCES

Barbe, W. B., Swassing, R. H., & Milone, M. N. 1979. *Teaching Through Modality Strengths: Concepts Practices*. Columbus, OH: Zaner-Bloser.

Brown, R. M. 1983. *Sudden Death*. New York, NY: Bantam.

Casey, B. J., Somerville, L. H., Gotlib, I. H., Ayduk, O., Franklin, N. T., Askren, M. K., Jonides, J., Berman, M. G., Wilson, N. L., Teslovich, T., Glover, G., Zayas, V., Mischel, W., & Shoda, Y. 2011. "Behavioral and Neural Correlates of Delay of Gratification 40 Years Later." *Proceedings of the National Academy of Sciences 108*(36), 14998–15003.

Constantinidou, F., & S. Baker. 2002. "Stimulus Modality and Verbal Learning Performance in Normal Aging." *Brain and Language 82*(3), 296–311.

Feng, M., J. Hawkins, J. Park, & G. Josep, G. n.d. What's Happening to My Body When I'm Sick? https://www.education.txstate.edu/ci/faculty/dickinson/PBI/PBIFall06/Disease/Content/LP3.htm.

Flavell, J. H. 1976. "Metacognitive Aspects of Problem Solving." In L. B. Resnick (ed.), *The Nature of Intelligence*, pp. 231–35. Hillsdale, NJ: Lawrence Erlbaum.

Green, E. L. 2019. "LeBron James Opened a School That Was Considered an Experiment. It's Showing Promise." *The New York Times*. https://www.nytimes.com/2019/04/12/education/lebron-james-school-ohio.html

James, W. 1890. *The Principles of Psychology: American Science Series-Advanced Course*. New York, NY: Henry Holt.

Kolb, D. A. 2015. *Experiential Learning: Experience as the Source of Learning and Development*. (2nd ed.). Upper Saddle River, NJ: Pearson Education.

Mallett, J. (May 6 and 7, 2019). *Frazz* [Syndicated Comic]. https://www.gocomics.com/frazz/2019/05/06 and https://www.gocomics.com/frazz/2019/05/07

Marzano, R. J. 1998. *A Theory-based Meta-analysis of Research on Instruction*. Aurora, CO: Mid-continent Regional Educational Laboratory.

Maxwell, J. C. 2007. *Failing Forward: Turning Mistakes into Stepping Stones for Success.* Nashville, TN: Thomas Nelson.

McGonigal, J. 2011. *Reality Is Broken: Why Games Make Us Better and How They Can Change the World.* New York, NY: Vintage.

McGonigal, J. 2016. *Superbetter: How a Gameful Life Can Make You Stronger, Happier, Braver and More Resilient.* New York, NY: HarperCollins.

McGuire, S. Y., & S. McGuire. 2016. *Teach Students How to Learn: Strategies You Can Incorporate into Any Course to Improve Student Metacognition, Study Skills, and Motivation.* Sterling, VA: Stylus.

Mehta, J., & S. Fine. 2019. "High School Doesn't Have to Be Boring." *The New York Times: Sunday Review* (March 31, 2019) 168.58, 283, 4.

Mischel, W. 2015. *The Marshmallow Test: Mastering Self-control.* New York, NY: Little, Brown, and Company.

Mumford, A. 1997. *Action Learning at Work.* Aldershot, UK: Gower.

Pashler, H., McDaniel, M., Rohrer, D., & Bjork, R. A. 2008. "Learning Styles: Concepts and Evidence." *Psychological Science in the Public Interest 3*, 105–119.

Schweinhart, L. J., J. Montie, Z. Xiang, W. S. Barnett, C. R. Belfield, & M. Nores. 2005. The High/Scope Perry Preschool Study Through Age 40: Summary, Conclusions, and Frequently Asked Questions. http://nieer.org/wp-content/uploads/2014/09/specialsummary_rev2011_02_2.pdf

Shoda, Y., W. Mischel, & P. K. Peake. 1990. "Predicting Adolescent Cognitive and Self-regulatory Competencies from Preschool Delay of Gratification: Identifying Diagnostic Conditions." *Developmental Psychology 26*(6), 978–86.

Veenman, M., & A. Desoete. (eds.). 2006. *Metacognition in Mathematics Education.* New York, NY: Nova Science Publishers.

Zimmerman, J. 2009. *Small Wonder: The Little Red Schoolhouse in History and Memory.* New Haven, CT: Yale University Press.

RESOURCES

Bell, K. 2018. *Shake up Learning: Practical Ideas to Move Learning from Static to Dynamic.* San Diego, CA: Dave Burgess Consulting.

Gustafson, B., & G. Couros. 2017. *Renegade Leadership: Creating Innovative Schools for Digital-age Students.* Thousand Oaks, CA: SAGE.

Mehta, J., & S. Fine. 2019. *In Search of Deeper Learning: The Quest to Remake the American High School.* Cambridge, MA: Harvard University Press.

Chapter Six

Student Behavioral Challenges

Few issues in school leadership are as divisive as the question of how to deal with student behavioral challenges. For many people, the answer involves greater understanding and nurturing. "They aren't really bad kids," proponents of this perspective will argue. "They just need someone in their lives who will listen to, believe in, and support them."

On the other side are those who argue that this approach is far too idealistic. "That's not how real classrooms work," advocates of a *tough love* strategy may argue. "Kids are not going to stop talking out of turn, bullying one another, and disrupting the class environment simply because we show that we care about them. We have to focus on the educational experience of the majority. We can't penalize most of the students—the ones who follow the rules—by coddling those who don't."

Like so many aspects of life that evoke strongly bimodal responses, the truth lies somewhere between these two extreme positions. School leaders *do* have to think of the interests of the majority of their students and *do* have an obligation to provide for a safe, well-managed, and highly effective learning environment.

At the same time, approaches that seek to suppress poor behavior by isolating and punishing those who act out may feel successful in the short term—they get the "troublemaker" out of the classroom and tie negative repercussions to specific acts—but they have a poor track record of making students better behaved in the long term.

The first step in addressing student behavioral challenges, therefore, is to recognize that student misconduct covers a very broad spectrum of activity. No reasonable person would suggest that talking out of turn should be handled in the same way as bringing a weapon into a classroom, and yet a surprising number of books on the topic of student behavior are written with the assumption that there is a standard approach or technique that should be adopted in all misconduct cases.

So, if teachers and school leaders are going to be effective in addressing disciplinary issues, the first question they need to ask is this: What sort of student behavioral challenge am I dealing with?

One time-effective way in which to begin this process is to conduct a quick behavioral triage, exploring which of the following categories best defines the issue:

- Is the student engaging in an activity that poses an immediate threat to the student himself/herself or others?
- Is the student engaging in an activity that, although it does not pose an immediate threat, could be detrimental to himself/herself or others in the long term?
- Is the student engaging in an activity that, although it does not pose an immediate or long-term threat, is interfering with the ability of other students to learn?
- Is the student engaging in an activity that, although it does not pose an immediate or long-term threat, is interfering with his or her own ability to learn?
- Is the student engaging in an activity that, although it does not pose any type of threat or interference with the pedagogical process, is annoying, irritating, or tiresome to me personally?

The best way to respond to each of these situations is different and so each category of behavior needs to be addressed individually.

BEHAVIOR THAT POSES AN IMMEDIATE THREAT

Activities that pose an immediate threat cross the line from being merely behavioral challenges to becoming genuine safety issues. As a result, many of the recommendations that were outlined in chapter 2 should be considered. Most schools have protocols for how teachers and administrators are to handle situations involving weapons on school property, fighting, and bullying.

The first priority in these situations is to follow this established protocol in order to ensure the health and safety of everyone involved. First, take active steps to make sure that other students are in the best possible location to protect themselves. If necessary, contact 911 and relevant resource officers at the school. Then

- remain calm and in control,
- be respectful but firm in your tone,

- be direct and repeat yourself as often as necessary, and
- inform other administrators about what is occurring and engage their assistance as appropriate.

Preserving the safety of students surpasses even the school's pedagogical mission in importance in situations where students pose an immediate threat to themselves or others. Your first priority has to be to secure the scene and deescalate the situation. Analysis of what caused the situation in the first place can come later.

The cornerstone of reducing disciplinary infractions is setting a high standard for interpersonal relations among all the school's stakeholders. School leaders can help set this standard and support effective classroom management through serving as positive role models, providing regular professional development to all members of the faculty and staff, and by insisting that the entire administrative team be highly visible on a daily basis.

The administrative team should also develop a comprehensive safety plan as recommended in chapter 2 and be sure that all members of the faculty and staff are trained in how best to manage any crisis situation.

Behaviors that pose an immediate threat call for serious sanctions to reinforce the message that these behaviors cannot be tolerated in school or elsewhere, demonstrate to victims that the situation has been taken seriously, and reduce the likelihood of a recurrence. Although these events may in their own ways provide teachable moments for the school, it is rarely regarded by parents and community members as sufficient to approach them only from a pedagogical perspective and not include some type of punishment. Since the violation of local, state, or federal laws may also be involved, additional punishments may be imposed beyond the level of the school itself.

BEHAVIOR THAT POSES A LONG-TERM THREAT

Activities that pose a long-term threat include such behaviors as cruel or aggressive teasing, body shaming, and low-level bullying. The children on the receiving end of these behaviors are unlikely to be in any immediate danger, although they may well be irritated or upset, but their self-esteem, satisfaction with the educational process, and overall well-being might suffer over time.

Behaviors that pose a long-term threat require quick intervention but not of the sort you might use if there were a risk of immediate violence. Administrators or teachers need to step in as soon as these behaviors are brought to their attention and make clear to everyone that this type of activity is not acceptable, either in terms of the school's culture or of societal values as a whole. Recommendations about what to do include the following:

- Listen carefully to how the students describe their perceptions of the situation and acknowledge their distress or anger.
- Identify the problem to make sure you understand it.
- If one or more students have brought the issue to your attention, don't demean them for "tattling," but, instead, praise them for confiding in you.
- Offer your assistance in resolving the matter.
- If appropriate, inform the students involved about any school resources that may be of help.
- Convey an attitude of support and understanding.
- If one or more of the students is upset, ask for permission to contact a family member or friend.

Of course, the best approach is to reduce the likelihood of these behavioral infractions *before* they occur. One of the primary responsibilities of the school leaders is to create an environment that promotes the success of all students, including their success as properly behaving members of their community.

A major key to creating a positive school environment is to prioritize the building of mutually supportive relationships. School leaders do so by example, developing strong, trusting, and mutual respectful relationships between themselves and members of the faculty and staff as well as external stakeholders. Those positive relationships then serve as the blueprint for how students are expected to interact with one another, their teachers, and all other members of the school community.

Nearly all schools have codes of conduct. But relatively few have developed *codes of expectations*. A code of conduct tells students what they *shouldn't* do, but a code of expectations helps teach students how they *should* behave. Effective codes of conduct are aspirational. Students (and, for that matter, faculty, staff, and administrators as well) won't always live *up* to those standards, but the code provides a guide to live *into*.

The code of conduct combined with a code of expectations provides all members of the school community with a clear example of what behavior is valued at the school and what consequences are likely to occur when those high standards aren't met. The school's values can complement its academic mission in a number of ways. Beginning in early grades and continuing through the end of high school, these codes are a natural complement to units on values clarification or exercises on character building.

For example, the Overcoming Obstacles life skills curriculum addresses the skills of communication, decision making, and goal setting and lends itself to values clarification and character development at both elementary and secondary levels of education. Values addressed in the Overcoming Obstacles life skills curriculum include empathy, mutual respect, teamwork, and citizenship taught through such processes as conflict resolution, the prevention of bullying, and problem solving (Overcoming Obstacles 2019).

Learning for Life is another program that involves grade-specific values clarification, focusing on the principles of respect, responsibility, honesty and trust, caring and fairness, perseverance, self-discipline, courage, and citizenship. Sample classroom activities in early childhood education include role-playing scenarios where good manners are required, reading and discussing *The Berenstain Bears Forget Their Manners* (Berenstain and Berenstain 1985), and circling illustrations that depict polite and responsible behaviors (Learning for Life, 2015).

Character Counts! provides practical strategies and tools to incorporate explorations of six values—caring, citizenship, trustworthiness, fairness, responsibility, and respect—into other classroom subjects and cocurricular activities (Character Counts! n.d.). The Capturing Kids' Hearts program of the Flippen Group takes a slightly different approach by seeking to address student engagement and behavior, not through ancillaries to the curriculum, but through a systematic approach to improving school culture by addressing the "invisible backpacks" that all members of a school community wear.

> Many of our students today come to school wearing invisible backpacks. They carry with them unreasonable expectations, stress from home, hunger, abuse, loneliness. We all know, and the research proves, that these items weigh heavily on students and can greatly impede their educational progress. We also know that if teachers can create a relational connection to students, or in Flippen Group terms, "Capture Kids' Hearts," performance goes way up, and behaviors greatly improve because kids want to be in school. Students are not the only ones with invisible backpacks. Teachers, staff, and administrators all have challenges they face as well. Some carry stress, overwhelming responsibilities, or unreasonable expectations of students and other staff members. . . . All campus educators can acquire specific socio-emotional learning techniques and classroom facilitation tools. Once equipped, they will be able to peak student interest, establish collaborative agreements of behavior in every classroom, create high performing groups, increase pro-social skills, create more time on-task, and increase student performance. (Capturing Kids' Hearts n.d.)

In other words, the program begins by recognizing that the pressures that can lead to behaviors that pose a long-term threat almost always arise outside the classroom and affect school leaders and faculty members no less than they do students. By recognizing these pressures and developing a school culture that addresses them in responsible, socially acceptable ways, Capturing Kids' Hearts seeks to decrease discipline referrals at the same time that it increases satisfaction rates of students and teachers alike with the school's learning environment.

As part of the program, teachers shake their students' hands as they come in the room and call each student by name on a daily basis. The goal is to set a model for what respectful social interactions look like and thus improve the relationships among students and between the faculty and students, with the aim of avoiding negative behaviors and increasing student attendance and graduation rates.

Strong working relationships between the school's internal stakeholders (students, teachers, and administrators) and its external stakeholders (parents, community members, and board members) create an atmosphere in which positive interactions are more likely to occur and in which behavioral expectations can be discussed. The school council and other existing advisory committees may provide useful advice on how different types of behavioral infractions should be addressed and, with the help of these groups and other outside agencies, a comprehensive approach to student behavior, including both a code of conduct and a code of expectations, can be developed.

But developing an approach isn't enough. It must also be communicated and followed. Discussions should be held about best practices to use in addressing different types of behavioral challenges. For all stakeholders to feel that a safe and mutually supportive school culture has been created, the approach should be continuously monitored, revised, practiced, and critiqued.

Sometimes teachers worry that, unless a student is engaging in a behavior that leads to immediate harm, they can't discuss their concerns with other faculty members or administrators because of the restrictions imposed by FERPA, the Family Educational Rights and Privacy Act of 1974. But these concerns are unfounded. FERPA does not prevent teachers from talking to another school employee about a student in distress if the goal is to assist the student or protect others in the school. So, school leaders should encourage teachers to use their best professional judgment to get themselves and their students the help and resources that they need.

BEHAVIOR THAT INTERFERES WITH THE ABILITY OF OTHER STUDENTS TO LEARN

Certain behavioral challenges don't pose either an immediate or long-term danger to students but do make the school's educational mission difficult. In the previous chapter, it was mentioned that the authors conducted a focus group of forty-seven active teachers at various types of schools. When this group was asked, "What are the top three behavioral challenges you feel your students encounter?" the majority of answers involved some form of mild to moderate class disruption. Although all schools are different, and it is indeed the case that certain schools witness more student-on-student violence than others, it's important to realize that the type of behavioral challenge most teachers are likely to face regularly involve disruptive rather than violent or threatening activity.

The types of classroom disruptions mentioned by teachers in the focus group included talking out of turn; a refusal to sit still and concentrate, pay attention, and remain focused; violating the personal space of others; distracting others; the inability to address negative feelings in a healthy way; acting on impulse; an unwillingness to accept consequences for one's actions; and a sense of entitlement or a belief that the rules don't apply to them.

Some of these perceptions are, at least in the opinion of some observers, possibly generational. Teachers who grew up and were training in an environment where the goal was to prepare students for work in a corporate or industrial workplace tend to place more emphasis on students remaining in their seats and listening quietly while the teacher speaks than teachers trained more recently who have an expectation that both educational and work environments will be dynamic, interactive, and team oriented rather than slow-paced, passive, and individual oriented.

Certainly, parallels may be found in the changing nature of popular media. For example, one study demonstrated that movies from 1935 to 2010 consistently grew shorter, more action oriented rather than dialogue oriented, and darker in emotional tone (Cutting, Brunick, DeLong, Iricinschi, and Candan 2011.) Nevertheless, it's a dangerous practice to approach generations in terms of stereotypes. All students are different and, if one student expects the classroom to be as fast-paced and rapidly changing as a video game, there is likely to be another who prefers long periods of intense focus on a single subject.

Moreover, even if certain differences in expectations can be regarded as generational, those differences are far from being the primary cause of behavioral challenges. Researchers have long demonstrated that attention span develops *in everyone* with age and that it's simply unreasonable to expect a third-grader, sixth-grader, and junior in high school to demonstrate the same capacity to pay attention for extended periods (Plude, Enns, and Brodeur 1994; Cowan, Nugent, Elliott, Ponomarev, and Saults 1999; Raffaelli, Crockett, and Shen 2005.)

Even so, there are practical steps that teachers and administrators can take to help students increase their attention span and decrease their likelihood of disrupting the learning process of other students.

Don't Keep Students in Their Seats for Too Long, Particularly in the Lower Grades

Students leave their seats and disrupt one another when they feel that they simply can't sit still any longer. Anticipate this challenge and incorporate it into pedagogical strategy. Physical activity doesn't have to be solely recreational, at least not all the time. Learning games, chanting or reciting concepts while marching, and other such activities can help to reinforce classroom concepts at the same time that they keep students active.

Break Tasks into Pieces and then Scaffold Those Steps

Students can become distracted while solving lengthy, multistep problems or learning complex procedures. Breaking these activities into self-contained steps and then combining those steps in an age-appropriate manner for the students' gradually lengthening attention span helps avoid disruptive classroom behavior by keeping the students more engaged.

> For example, if the task is to put together a visual report about the state of Texas that includes economy, geography, culture and history components, you may want to have the child focus on one component at a time. Only when one component is finished are instructions given for completing the next component. Once all component parts have been completed, instructions are then given as to how the individual parts are to be combined to create the visual report. (Tips for Increasing a Student's Attention Span 2019)

Make the Lesson Inquiry Based

Students are much more likely to remain engaged in an activity for longer periods if they view that activity as solving a mystery or telling a story. Doing so provides them with a reason to care and to see an immediate connection between the lesson and their own existing interests. In their book *Made to Stick* (2010), Chip and Dan Heath describe how Robert Cialdini, a social scientist at Arizona State University, transformed a dull lesson on the rings of Saturn into a compelling and engaging lesson by turning it into a mystery.

> How can we account for what is perhaps the most spectacular planetary feature in our solar system, the rings of Saturn? There's nothing else like them. What are the rings of Saturn made of anyway? And then he deepened the mystery further by asking, "How could three internationally acclaimed groups of scientists come to wholly different conclusions on the answer?" One, at Cambridge University, proclaimed they were gas; another group, at MIT, was convinced they were made up of dust particles; while the third, at CalTech, insisted they were comprised of ice crystals. How could this be, after all, each group was looking at the same thing. right? So, what was the answer? (Heath and Heath 2010, pp. 80–81)

Other ideas for how to help develop longer attention spans include using humor as a pedagogical technique, incorporating student preferences into the design of a lesson plan, and relating lessons to items in the news and real-life problems.

Your goal as a school leader is not necessarily to mandate any of these strategies but rather to encourage teachers to be creative in terms of how they approach student engagement. No single approach will be appropriate for all subjects, all grade levels, or all teaching styles, but letting teachers know that you support innovative pedagogical strategies designed to maximize student engagement is a key element in helping reduce behaviors that interfere with the ability of other students to learn.

BEHAVIOR THAT INTERFERES WITH A STUDENT'S OWN ABILITY TO LEARN

Sometimes the problem isn't that a student is disrupting others but that he or she in engaging in activities that get in his or her own way toward progress. For example, the teachers in the authors' focus group described the challenge of educating students who have a difficult time focusing on a task to completion, struggle with staying on task when working in groups, are easily distracted, and are unable to take responsibility for their own learning.

As in the previous section, many of these challenges are the result of short attention spans either due to the student's age, the impact of culture and popular entertainment, or both. But other behaviors that interfere with a student's own ability to learn may be the result of learning disabilities, hyperactivity, attention-deficit disorder, and other conditions that pose individual challenges.

504 plans, so called because they are described under Section 504 of the Federal Rehabilitation Act of 1973, outline the accommodations and assistance that must be provided to students who have a diminished ability to access learning in a traditional educational setting due to a learning-, behavior- or health-related condition. An IEP or individualized education program specifies the services and supplementary aids that schools are to provide students with special needs through the twelfth grade.

But 504 plans and IEPs are not a panacea. For example, while parents can request that a child be evaluated to determine whether a 504 plan is appropriate, they can't require it.

> [A] school district does not have to refer or evaluate a child under Section 504 solely upon parental demand. The key to a referral is whether the school district staff suspects that the child is suffering from a mental or physical impairment that substantially limits a major life activity and is in need of either regular education with supplementary services or special education and related services. (Durheim, 2018)

Moreover, even though public school districts in the United States are required to offer the accommodations outlined in a 504 plan or IEP, private schools have much greater leeway and may decide that the services specified in these plans are not reasonable in light of their resources.

An even greater challenge with 504 plans and IEPs is that, even in public schools, class size and limited resources can make their implementation extremely difficult. In a class with twenty-five students, if five students require special accommodation, the time a teacher devotes to other students (a number of whom may have their own special needs even without a 504 plan or IEP) can become very limited. What, then, can school leaders do in order to help teachers address those behaviors that interfere with their students' own ability to learn in light of these limitations of time and other resources?

Remind Teachers That Humiliation Is Counterproductive as a Pedagogical Method

In the memorable phrase that Annette Breaux and Todd Whitaker introduce in *50 Ways to Improve Student Behavior* (2015), humiliation breeds retaliation.

> Do you now remember the teacher who humiliated you as one of your favorites? Of course you don't. In fact, most adults will admit to still harboring feelings of resentment and dislike for teachers who humiliated them many years ago. They can still conjure up the same feelings as if the act of humiliation happened yesterday. That's how powerful and damaging humiliation can be. No one ever says, "Boy, when Mrs. Crabapple humiliated me, it surely made me want to be a better student. I thank her for that even today. . . ." What Mrs. Crabapple did not realize was that humiliation never works. In fact, it causes resentment and embarrassment, and it often leads to retaliation. (Breaux and Whitaker 2015, p. 67)

In other words, while "shutting an overactive student down" may bring peace to the classroom in the short term, it may lead to even greater disruptions in the future. A child who is only interfering with his or her own educational process today may end up interfering with that of many other students tomorrow.

Discourage Teachers from Using You and Other School Leaders as "Enforcers"

Being sent to the principal's office has become almost synonymous with punishment for poor behavior. But when teachers threaten students with a visit to the principal or vice principal if they continue to disrupt the classroom, it causes more problems than it solves. First, it suggests that teachers themselves aren't empowered to maintain order in the classroom; only school leaders can do that. The most effective role of the school leader is to advise teachers on the appropriate ways of dealing with classroom disruption within that particular school's culture and then backing teachers up when they enforce the code of conduct. Second, it suggests that school leaders (and by extension all figures of authority, including parents and police officers) aren't there to protect people; they're there to punish them. The result can be that students become more secretive of misconduct—whether their own or that of others—and deprive school leaders of opportunities to take advantage of teachable moments before they become genuine problems.

Encourage Teachers to Serve as Good Role Models When They Respond to Classroom Disruption

If a teacher responds angrily to an angry student, it sends a message that acting out in anger is an appropriate response. If a teacher overreacts to a student who is overreacting, it exacerbates the situation rather than calming it. Breaux and Whitaker (2015) recommend that teachers ask themselves six questions as a checklist whenever they need to deal with a disruptive student.

1. Do I take extra care to be a constant role model of courtesy in all situations?
2. Do I appear enthusiastic and motivated while I am teaching?
3. Even when I have to reprimand a student, do I do it in a calm, controlled manner, treating the student with dignity?
4. Am I respectful at all times?
5. Do my students think of me as a happy person?
6. Does each student know that I like him/her? (Breaux and Whitaker 2015, p. 75–76)

Rita Platt, a National Board-Certified Teacher, offers the following advice in dealing with students whose behavior interferes with the ability of others to learn.

> When students misbehave, they are communicating with us. . . . Try to listen. Get to the bottom of the need they are trying to meet. Is the student seeking attention? A sense of control? A release from fear of failure? Once you identify the need, you can work to proactively ward off poor behavior. . . . Misbehavior is an opportunity to *teach*. That's a good thing! That's what we do! The kids in our classes are going to run the world when we're old. We need to help them learn strong character traits such as respect, cooperation, assertion, empathy, and self-control. It may be hard, but it will pay off for *all* of us in the long run. (Platt 2018)

BEHAVIOR THAT'S MERELY ANNOYING, IRRITATING, OR TIRESOME TO YOU

We all have our pet peeves, behaviors that, for whatever reason, seem to annoy us more than they annoy other people. And in any community, the sheer number of people with whom we interact means that the odds of someone engaging in one of our personal pet peeves increases. But teachers and administrators have to be on their guard against confusing personal pet peeves with genuine behavioral problems when students engage in these behaviors.

There are two questions that must always be asked when a teacher or school leader suspects that a student is engaging in inappropriate behavior: "What is the actual harm that is being done?" and "What is the specific behavior that is causing that harm?"

In each of the four categories of student behavioral challenges explored above, it is clear that some tangible harm was indeed being done. The student was causing either immediate or long-term danger to himself or herself or others or was interfering with his or her own learning process or that of others. It was thus possible to identify the specific behavior causing that harm and address it in appropriate ways.

But when a student is only behaving in a way that irritates the adult observer, it is far more difficult to identify an actual harm that results. Sometimes, of course, it may indeed be possible to say that the behavior is causing a problem. It's not inappropriate to say things like, "I'm sorry, Kristi, but I have a bad headache today, and when you tap your pencil that way, it makes my headache worse. I need you to refrain from doing that, at least for today."

At other times, however, the student's behavior merely involves one of the observer's personal pet peeves. Perhaps the student is inconsistent, loving a game one day and indifferent to it the next. Or perhaps the student feels compelled to critique the teacher's style of dress or to show the teacher some new skill he or she has developed, even if it's not at all relevant to the course material. Depending on the teacher's sensibilities, these activities may be annoying, irritating, or tiresome, but they rarely produce any tangible harm.

Depending on the child's age, it may be possible to use the occasion as an opportunity to discuss acceptable group behavior and the fact that certain activities annoy some people but not others. On the whole, however, it's important for school leaders to set an appropriate example that behaviors of this kind do not rise to the level of being problems and therefore do not need to be addressed in the same way as a genuine behavioral challenge.

FINAL REMARKS

At the beginning of this chapter, it was noted that the issue of student behavioral challenges is sometimes quite divisive. Some people believe that lapses in behavior should be dealt with through understanding and kindness, while others believe that this type of response reinforces poor behavior rather than eliminating it.

As should now be clear, this bimodal perspective tends to arise when people think of student misbehavior as monolithic. Some behavioral challenges are minor enough that they *should* be regarded as teachable moments, whereas others cause or threaten danger so significant that they must be dealt with far more aggressively. The role of the school leader should be to help teachers and other stakeholders understand that not all lapses in behavior are alike and that student behavioral challenges are situations in which it's best to respond *equitably* even if not *equally*.

It's not equitable to treat an accidental harm in the same way as an intentional harm, and it's not equitable to treat a careless accident in the same way as a completely random and unpreventable accident. Responding equally in all these situations doesn't help teach students how to act better in group settings or how to respond when they themselves engage in an activity that causes problems for others.

In many ways, these lessons about behavior are connected seamlessly with other lessons the students are learning about critical thinking, community values, and personal responsibility, lessons that can easily be undermined if teachers and administrators punish any infraction, regardless of its severity, in the same way.

A CASE STUDY ON STUDENT BEHAVIORAL CHALLENGES

Imagine that one of the teachers in your school stops by one day to ask for advice about how to deal with Felix Cited, a student who has been assigned to the teacher this year. During your conversation, you learn the following about Felix's behavior:

- He has a tendency to get out of his seat and walk around the room during times when the students are supposed to be working independently at their desks.
- He has a hard time being quiet and will often talk to one or more of the students around him when the students are supposed to be paying attention to the teacher or what another student is saying.
- When called upon, Felix sometimes gives responses that ramble or that aren't clearly relevant to the topic being discussed.

- He often acts in ways that seem impulsive or random.
- At the end of the day, Felix sometimes mindlessly pushes other students aside in his desire to get outside first.

What advice do you give the teacher?

DISCUSSION OF THE CASE STUDY

The case study of Felix Cited calls to mind the principle that *before school leaders can address a problem, they must first diagnose the cause of the problem*.

To begin with, no information is provided in the case study of Felix's age. If he's an elementary school student, the issue may largely be one of natural development. As was discussed in this chapter, attention span and the ability to focus increase in most children as they age. If Felix is a high school student, however, he may well be suffering from attention-deficit disorder (ADD), perhaps coupled with hyperactivity (attention-deficit/hyperactivity order [ADHD]).

For this reason, depending on Felix's age, a good place to begin might be to recommend testing to determine whether his inability to remain in his seat, be quiet, and pay attention to course material might derive from a condition that is independent of normal growth and development. If that is the case, an IEP might be developed to address his particular need.

If testing suggests that Felix is developing normally or does not appear to have ADD, ADHD, or a similar disorder, then some of the activities recommended in this chapter on how to increase a student's attention span might be in order.

A good place to begin is a private conversation with Felix in which he's reminded of the school's values about not engaging in activities that harm other members of the community. He may not be aware that his impulsivity and chatter interfere with the educational activities of his classmates, but, if reminded of this issue in an age-appropriate manner, his behavior may improve.

This conversation might start with the impact that his thoughtless pushing of other students has when he's leaving class. Felix might be asked, "How does it feel when other students push *you* on their way out of the classroom, Felix? Won't your friends feel the same way when you push *them*?"

In addition, encouraging the teacher to rethink his or her lesson plans so that *none* of the students are required to remain in one place for too long might be in order. Felix may simply be doing what other students in the class are sorely tempted to do because the way in which they're being taught is requiring them to sit still longer than can reasonably be expected at their age.

By incorporating some physical activity into the teacher's lesson plans, Felix's behavioral challenges may decrease at the same time that overall student performance increases.

Finally, improved lesson scaffolding and the introduction of additional inquiry-based instruction may help Felix improve his focus by causing him to become more engaged with the course material. At the moment, he may find conversations with other students more interesting that the material being taught, but that situation may change if the lessons begin to tell a story, solve a mystery, or help him address real-world problems to which he can relate.

KEY POINTS IN THIS CHAPTER

- The topic of student behavioral challenges covers a very wide range of activity. When people suggest that there's only one effective way to deal with poor behavior, they're usually thinking of only a relatively small subset of these challenges.
- Behavior that causes immediate danger for the student himself or herself or others must be dealt with urgently, and the first thing to keep in mind is the safety of all members of the school community. In these instances, learning lessons from the event can wait. Maintaining security must come first.
- Behavior that poses a long-term threat is best prevented by clearly conveying the school's values and behavioral goals to all members of the community and by complementing a code of conduct with an aspirational code of expectations. When these expectations are not met, the inappropriate behavior should be stopped immediately and then followed with a renewed lesson on why the community's values are important and must be respected.
- Behavior that interferes with the ability of other students to learn should be addressed promptly but not treated in the same way as behavior that causes an immediate danger or threat to safety. These situations should regularly be regarded as teachable moments in terms of appropriate interpersonal behavior. They should also cause the teacher to reflect on the possibility that the course material might benefit from improved scaffolding or the incorporation of inquiry-based lessons so as to promote better student engagement.
- Behavior that interferes with a student's own ability to learn should be addressed in a manner that assists the child without humiliating the child. If a student becomes increasingly frustrated by his or her apparent ability to master a skill or complete a unit, care should be taken to avoid having the student conclude, "I'm just not good at math," or "I'm not one of those

people who can learn foreign languages." This type of behavioral problem in particular is a way of students communicating to teachers and administrators that one of their educational needs isn't being met. By paying close attention to the circumstances in which that behavior arises, you can often determine what that unmet need is and develop a positive intervention that both helps the student learn and improves his or her behavior.

* Behavior that's merely annoying, irritating, or tiresome to teachers or administrators usually doesn't pass the test of causing an actual and tangible harm. It may merely relate to a pet peeve that the teacher or administrator has and, if it does, is probably best ignored rather than regarded as a serious behavioral challenge.

REFERENCES

Berenstain, S., & J. Berenstain. 1985. *The Berenstain Bears Forget Their Manners*. New York, NY: Random House.

Breaux, A., & T. Whitaker. 2015. *50 Ways to Improve Student Behavior: Simple Solutions to Complex Challenges*. New York, NY: Routledge.

Character Counts! (n.d.) https://charactercounts.org

Cowan, N., L. D. Nugent, E. M. Elliott, I. Ponomarev, & J. S. Saults. 1999. "The Role of Attention in the Development of Short-term Memory: Age Differences in the Verbal Span of Apprehension." *Child Development 70*(5), 1082–1097.

Cutting, J. E., K. L. Brunick, J. E. DeLong, C. Iricinschi, & A. Candan. 2011. "Quicker, Faster, Darker: Changes in Hollywood Film over 75 Years." *I-perception 2*(6), 569–76.

Durheim, M. 2018. "A Parent's Guide to Section 504 in Public School." https://www.greatschools.org/gk/articles/section-504-2/

The Flippen Group: Capturing Kids' Hearts. (n.d.) https://flippengroup.com/education-solutions/capturing-kids-hearts/

Heath, C., & D. Heath. 2010. *Made to Stick: Why Some Ideas Take Hold and Others Come Unstuck*. New York, NY: Random House.

Learning for Life: Early Childhood. 2015. http://learning.learningforlife.org/programs/chardev-overview/chardev-ec/

Overcoming Obstacles: The Curriculum. 2019. https://www.overcomingobstacles.org/curriculum/

Platt, R. 2018. "10 Tips to Maintain Positive Student Behavior." https://www.middleweb.com/38909/10-tips-to-maintain-positive-student-behavior/

Plude, D. J., J. T. Enns, & D. Brodeur. 1994. The Development of Selective Attention: A Life-span Overview. *Acta Psychologica* 86, 227–72.

Raffaelli, M., L. J. Crockett, & Y. L. Shen. 2005. "Developmental Stability and Change in Self-regulation from Childhood to Adolescence." *The Journal of Genetic Psychology* 166(1), 54–75.

Tips for Increasing a Student's Attention Span: Education Corner. 2019. https://www.educationcorner.com/tips-for-increasing-attention-span.html

RESOURCES

Bowen, J. M., W. R. Jenson, & E. Clark. 2004. *School-Based Interventions for Students with Behavior Problems*. New York, NY: Kluwer Academic/Plenum Publishers.

Dupper, D. R. 2010. *A New Model of School Discipline: Engaging Students and Preventing Behavior Problems*. New York, NY: Oxford University Press.

Flick, G. L. 2011. *Understanding and Managing Emotional and Behavior Disorders in the Classroom.* Boston, MA: Pearson.

Kampwirth, T. J., & K. M. Powers. 2016. *Collaborative Consultation in the Schools: Effective Practices for Students with Learning and Behavior Problems.* (5th ed.) Boston, MA: Pearson.

Kern, L., M. P. George, & M. D. Weist. 2016. *Supporting Students with Emotional and Behavioral Problems: Prevention and Intervention Strategies.* Baltimore, MD: Paul H. Brookes Publishing Co.

Kerr, M. M., & C. M. Nelson. 2010. *Strategies for Addressing Behavior Problems in the Classroom.* (6th ed.). Boston, MA: Pearson.

Sprick, R. S. 1985. *Discipline in the Secondary Classroom: A Problem-by-Problem Survival Guide.* West Nyack, NY: Center for Applied Research in Education.

Chapter Seven

Effective Student Evaluation

In chapter 4, two important points were made about faculty and staff evaluation. The first is that school systems tend to overemphasize summative evaluation when diagnostic, formative, and summative-formative evaluations are often more effective at achieving the results that school leaders want. The second is that short, intensive student orientation sessions are less successful than a well-designed first-year experience program, and thus that first-year experience programs should also be used instead of brief orientation sessions when onboarding new members of the faculty and staff.

In this chapter, we'll return to the distinction among diagnostic, formative, summative, and summative-formative evaluations and argue that a lesson learned first about the faculty and staff, that there should be less summative and more formative evaluation, should also be applied to students.

Sharp differences of opinion have arisen over the value and validity of standardized tests, no matter whether those tests are nationally normed—such as the SAT (which originally stood for "Scholastic Aptitude Test" and now is simply a brand identifier, not an acronym) and the ACT (which originally stood for "American College Testing" and now is also simply a brand identifier)—or state-developed—such as the California Assessment of Student Performance and Progress and the Tennessee Comprehensive Assessment Program.

These state-developed tests are required in American public schools by US Public Law 107-110 in its current form as the Every Student Succeeds Act. Schools and districts that do not offer standardized tests are ineligible for federal funding. Advocates of standardized tests argue that they help provide greater consistency of educational opportunities, set high standards, and help provide a focus for a school's curriculum.

Opponents of the tests argue that they are unnecessarily stressful to children, discriminate against non-English speakers and students with special needs, are not nearly as objective as they claim to be, and become de facto "teacher achievement tests," not the measures of student achievement they were intended to be.

The questions raised about standardized tests can also be raised about many aspects of how students are evaluated in general. For example, what message are educators sending to young minds when education seems to be primarily about preparing for the next major test? Are we taking away their creativity, their ability to be risk takers and problem solvers?

Many people today complain that the "younger generation" (and there have been complaints about the younger generation for as long as there have been generations) can't work independently, wants to be rewarded "just for showing up," and appears to be stressed out by situations that those before them simply took in stride. But these impressions are simply part of a stereotype, and, like all stereotypes, they conceal the rich diversity of ability and experience that teachers encounter in their classes every day. How can that diversity be reflected in a single standardized test? And does it really encourage students to work independently, increase their intrinsic motivation, and deal more effectively with the pressures of life when school seems to be a nonstop sequence of meaningless hurdles, the only result of which appears to be to divide people (including their own teachers) into classes of "successes" and "failures"?

Make no mistake about it: competition can be healthy. But in order for success in a competition to mean something, it's essential for the right training to be provided before the competition and for the challenge involved to be truly meaningful. Just as too many outcomes assessments in schools are ineffective because they "assess the assessable" rather than the factors that are really important, too much of our current approach to student grading simply "evaluates the evaluatable" instead of addressing what we really want our schools to accomplish. To put it bluntly, most student evaluation systems today deserve a failing grade.

HOW TRADITIONAL EVALUATION FAILS STUDENTS

A major reason why so many problems exist with the evaluation system used in schools is that it's not consistent over time. In their primary years, students are encouraged to draw, create, and conduct science experiments without the pressure of focusing on the end product. During this time, many teachers observe that their students flourish academically and are socioemotionally well adjusted.

At this stage in the educational process, when something doesn't go right during a science experiment, a child will typically say something like, "Well, I guess that didn't work. Let's try something else." Rarely do teachers hear young science students say, "That didn't work! I'm not going to try anymore!" Instead, they tend to be excited about exploring new ideas, even when they're not initially successful at mastering them. They want to find out what else can work to find a solution. Wouldn't it be amazing if we could transfer that mind-set to apply to all of the students' subject areas?

In middle school, however, the educational focus in most schools changes. From this point on, instruction becomes much more goal oriented rather than process oriented.

- Middle school teachers often see their job as "getting students ready for high school."
- High school teachers often see their job as "getting students ready for college."
- College teachers often see their job as "getting students ready for the job market."

As a result, the goal of education becomes less about personal growth and development and more about simply reaching the next level.

In psychology, there is a phenomenon known as *destination addiction*. This phenomenon occurs when people are never content with what they're doing right now but believe (falsely) that they'll finally become happy when at last they get that big promotion, buy that splendid new house, read the latest self-help book, earn yet another graduate degree, or something similar.

In many ways, schools suffer from their own type of destination addiction. It's not just about "getting students out the door" with a diploma or degree (even though politicians sometimes speak as though graduation, not the learning that entitles students to graduate, is a school's "end product"), but rather about the feeling school leaders often have that their success is measured by whether they can "get students ready" for the next hurdle in the educational process.

This tendency has a significant impact in how students are taught and evaluated. Teachers speak about the need to "cover" a certain amount of material, not about the students' need to master that material. They talk about "getting through" certain units, almost as though those units are unsavory parts of town that they have to travel through to get home safely. And they implement evaluation systems that cause students to fixate on the score or grade rather than what they gained from their learning.

It's no wonder then that many students, after they graduate, take courses in mindfulness and that meditation and yoga have flourished in recent years: Their lives have felt like a continual series of ladders where, just as soon as they've reached the top of one level, they discover that they're merely at the bottom of the next level. They are hungry for opportunities that allow them to be "in the moment" because their school systems never allowed them that luxury.

The paradox is that, by focusing exclusively on the "goal" of education, schools have lost sight of what that goal really should be. By defining success only as a certain score on an exam, they have increased pressure on students, parents, teachers, and administrators to make sure that "no child is left behind" by failing to achieve that score. And so, by not allowing students to fail and recover repeatedly from failure, traditional evaluation sets students up for even more serious failure in the future.

A BETTER APPROACH TO STUDENT EVALUATION

These problems can be avoided if school leaders work cooperatively with teachers to *focus on process more than product*. Doing so will not be easy. All too often legislators with very little background in child development or pedagogical methods set the journey for today's students. A familiar maxim among school leaders is that *everyone thinks they know how to run a school simply because they've* been *to school*. But, in many cases, the very efforts that legislatures and school boards make to improve education—no matter how well intended those efforts may be—end up getting in the way of our students' education.

Nevertheless, that effort is both necessary and worthwhile. By focusing on process over product, teachers help students value their educational journey, not just their "arrival" at the next stage of their lives. They produce better understanding with less stress, teach accountability and responsibility along the way, and foster student agency.

But the objection may arise: "That all may sound good. Nevertheless, results really do matter. The approach you're recommending sounds a bit too much like participation trophies and prizes for attendance, which is exactly what schools ought to be getting away from. When students get out into 'the real world,' they'll be judged on what they can produce, not on how much they enjoyed producing it."

Objections of this kind stem from a confusion between *evaluation* and *scoring*. Even in what people so frequently call "the real world," a great deal of evaluation is done that has very little to do with assigning a specific score. Many types of annual employee appraisals, for example, either don't assign scores at all or merely distinguish between performance that either meets or did not meet expectations. A substantial amount of appraisal that occurs in the workplace is actually *narrative evaluation*, which might be given in written form or might merely be conveyed orally.

In the type of narrative evaluation that occurs in the workplace, a supervisor goes through the various assignments the employee was given, highlights what the employee did well, summarizes what the employee did that was less successful, and offers suggestions for improvement. The Performance Resource Center provides the following example of how a narrative evaluation might be given to someone who was hired to work as a receptionist.

> Clarence works well under pressure and handles phone calls efficiently and effectively. His ability to stay on top of both calls and in-person visitors is a bonus, and several clients have commented on how polite and helpful he is. On occasion Clarence has misdirected calls, resulting in a few customers feeling they've gotten the runaround. This is probably due to not having had the roles of staff properly explained to him. (Narrative Method For Tracking and Documenting Employee Contributions 2018)

If evaluations of this sort are what students will receive after they leave school, it actually does them a disservice not to provide more narrative evaluation while the students are still in school.

It's certainly not necessary to replace every score or letter grade with a narrative evaluation, but it can be very beneficial for teachers to reduce the amount of scoring and grading they do and to replace some of this classification-based evaluation with narratives.

Leah Alcala, a seventh- and eighth-grade math teacher at King Middle School in Berkeley, California, explains what happens when teachers rely too much on grading and scoring: "What I was finding when I was handing back tests the old way, where I put a grade on it, was kids would look at their grade, decide whether they were good at math or not, and put the test away and never look at it again" (Schwartz 2018).

Students start identifying themselves as "B students" or "C students" and stop looking at assignments, quizzes, and tests as opportunities to grow; they see them only as corroboration that they're either a "smart kid" or a "dumb kid." Narrative evaluation can change all that.

Of course, shifting student evaluation from letter grades or numeric scores to narrative evaluation, at least in part, is a significant undertaking. It begins with providing the proper training and support for teachers and encouraging their buy-in. Narrative evaluation is a powerful pedagogical tool, but several factors can limit its effectiveness:

- Insufficient teacher training
- Inadequate time to engage in the process
- Resistance from parents, board members, and legislators who don't understand the process

In order to reduce the impact of these factors, there are several important steps school leaders can take.

TRAINING AND SUPPORT FOR TEACHERS

The idea of using narrative evaluations instead of scores and grades may seem so unfamiliar to many teachers that they may need special training in order to use this technique effectively. They may assume that narrative evaluation is suitable only for formative evaluation, while believing that assigning some type of number or letter to student performance is essential for there to be any kind of summative evaluation. It's important for the faculty to understand, therefore, that narrative evaluation is still evaluation; it's merely an approach to evaluation that doesn't bring with it all the problems associated with traditional grading.

Effective training in and support for the use of narrative evaluation can begin with an explanation of how this approach to performance appraisal flows directly from the setting of learning objectives. For example, let's suppose that the following is a unit objective set by a teacher of second-grade math:

> Students will master strategies of subtraction where the minuend, subtrahend, and difference are all less than or equal to 1,000. The strategies adopted will enable the students to understand when regrouping would be necessary and when they could subtract without regrouping. Students will participate in "regrouping relays" where breaking down the various steps involved in this process will be practiced and teamwork in problem solving will be encouraged. Students will review the skill of telling time by timing these activities to the second and thus understanding the concept of elapsed time in real-life situations. Students will then use these skills to examine their daily plans and identify the time both in digital and analog forms of each activity and calculate the elapsed time between those activities. Based on assessments conducted during the prior unit, mental math with fact fluency in addition (0–20) and multiplication (0–10) continues to be an area that students are still working on to improve, so additional exercises in these areas will be performed.

Following this unit, the teacher might write the following narrative evaluation for a student that we'll call Cy Burnett:

> Cy is an enthusiastic mathematician. He continues to elevate the level of group discussions and is eager to share his strategy and thought process with others. Cy has grown in his ability to check his work for accuracy, which has aided him in the ability to tackle multiple-step word problems. While completing multiple-step word problems remains a task that he finds challenging, Cy is now more consistent in his approach than was observed during the previous unit. Progress, while still encountering a certain degree of challenge, is also

true of Cy's work with addition or subtraction equations that require regrouping. His progress to date suggests, however, that these skills will continue to improve with more practice. During the project involving elapsed time skills and the students' daily plans, Cy was able appropriately to anticipate, label, and identify times to the hour, half hour, and minute. His application of skills through performance demonstrates thorough understanding of telling and measuring time in all areas that were assessed. In the next unit, Cy will be encouraged to take more risks when solving problems because he has shown that his ability to work through difficult problems often improves when he tests out new approaches.

After reading an evaluation like that, it becomes easy to see how much better everyone—future teachers, parents, and even Cy himself—will understand what Cy has learned and where he still needs to make progress than if all the teacher assigned was a score like 86 or a letter grade like a B.

It's also clear from this example how teachers can learn to make these narratives truly evaluative, not a mere listing of what the student has done. The teacher doesn't just praise the student when successful; the teacher also notes where challenges exist and (of even greater importance) what should be done about those challenges.

This opportunity for continual growth of skills continues when teachers discuss these narrative evaluations with their students in one-on-one conferences. During this conference, the teacher asks the student questions like

- What do you feel you excelled in during the last exercise/unit/term?
- In which areas do you feel you could continue to grow?
- Do you believe that you put in 100 percent effort as you completed your work?
- What do you think you might do differently during the next exercise/unit/term?

These conversations help reinforce the advice provided in the written narrative and model the process of self-reflection teachers want to develop in their students. By modeling, encouraging self-reflection, and leading students in candid self-assessments, the teachers are empowering students to become responsible for their own learning.

PROVIDING ADEQUATE TIME FOR EVALUATION

As a school incorporates more and more narrative evaluation into its appraisal of student work, teachers are likely to feel that the biggest obstacle to embracing this approach is the time it takes. Like any new technique, however, narrative evaluation may take more time at first when it is a new and unfamiliar process, but teachers become much more efficient at it over time.

In addition, it's appropriate for school leaders to ask teachers and department heads, if there is general agreement that narrative assessment is a valuable expenditure of time, which activities schools are requiring of teachers that are less valuable and, thus, able to be delegated to staff members or teachers' aides (or eliminated from people's workload entirely).

In addition, time for narrative evaluations may be saved, at least when teachers are first becoming familiar with the technique, by encouraging the writer to begin, not with a blank piece of paper, but with a template. For example, the sample evaluation of Cy Burnett presented earlier might have begun with the following template that the teacher adapts according to his or her observation of each student.

> [NAME] is a[n] [EVALUATIVE TERM] mathematician. S/he continues to [STATE AREA OF CONTINUED PROGRESS] and is [STATE ADDITIONAL STRENGTH]. [NAME] has grown in [STATE ANOTHER AREA OF PROGRESS]. While [STATE A CHALLENGE] remains an area that s/he finds challenging, [NAME] is [DESCRIBE STUDENT'S LEVEL OF PROGRESS WITH THIS CHALLENGE]. [IDENTIFY AN ADDITIONAL CHALLENGE.]. His/her progress to date suggests, however, that [PREDICT LIKELY RATE OF PROGRESS IN DEALING WITH THESE CHALLENGES]. During the project involving [NAME SPECIFIC PROJECT FROM UNIT], [NAME] was able appropriately to [STATE WHAT STUDENT DID PROPERLY]. His/her application of skills through performance demonstrates [EVALUATIVE CONCLUSION]. In the next unit, [NAME] will be encouraged to [SET SPECIFIC GOAL].

Most teachers find that, as they become more proficient in writing narrative evaluations, these templates become less necessary, and they are able to move directly from a unit plan to a student's assessment very quickly. In the meantime, however, the use of templates (which can be done either individually by the teacher or as a discipline-specific group within a professional learning community, a concept that will be discussed in chapter 10) both helps teachers learn how to write effective narrative assessments and saves them time.

COMMUNICATING THE VALUE OF NARRATIVE ASSESSMENT

While teachers may sometimes be reluctant to adopt narrative evaluation at first, the vast majority of them usually see the advantages of this approach rather quickly. The same thing cannot be said, however, of parents, school boards, and legislators who often find the replacement of many letter grades and scores with narrative evaluation to be a more radical change than they're comfortable with.

One way of communicating the value of narrative evaluation is to demonstrate its effectiveness in terms noneducators can understand. That data may be provided by trends in the standardized tests that schools are still required to give, but it can be provided even more powerfully by the students themselves.

When parents, board members, and legislators hear children articulate what they've learned, how they've learned it, and what they need to do next, they often understand just how powerful a technique narrative evaluation can be. If they ask a student from a school using traditional methods, "How good of a student are you?" they're likely to get answers like, "I'm an A student," or, "I'm a pretty good student."

When the same question is posed to students who have become familiar with narrative evaluation, they're likely to receive a far more nuanced and informative answer. Students don't just talk about the results of the learning process; they also talk about the pathways that led them to those results and how they can continue to make even greater progress in the future. As the old saying goes, "the proof of the pudding is in the eating" when it comes to the effectiveness of narrative evaluation.

Another approach to explaining the value of narrative evaluation to external constituents can be to point out that several universities, including some highly prestigious and selective universities, have also replaced traditional grading systems with narratives. The highly selective New College of Florida has used narrative evaluation since its inception and explains its value as follows:

> Professors at New College provide narrative evaluations instead of grades for each course or project you complete. That's because we believe that detailed feedback on your individual strengths and weaknesses—as well as suggestions for improvement and further study—are much more valuable than a mere letter grade. Through this process, faculty get to know students very well and are able to provide you with useful, informative feedback on your studies. Faculty can really look at your work holistically, rather than assigning an arbitrary grade that doesn't tell the whole story. Does the absence of grades impede entry to graduate school or your ability to get a job? Not at all! Narrative evaluations actually allow faculty to write strong, detailed recommendation letters for graduate school applications, scholarships and employment. About 80 percent of New College alumni go on to graduate school within six years of graduating. For the 2010 graduating class, 86 percent of graduates who applied to a Ph.D. program were accepted, and 100 percent who applied to law school got in. ("We're Different By Design" 2019)

In Washington, The Evergreen State College also uses narrative evaluations for many of the same reasons and with the same desirable outcomes.

[At Evergreen State,] the narrative evaluation is a dialogue. You'll get more feedback with how well you're doing, so you know where to go next, and what you're prepared for. The level of detail in an evaluation can go far beyond a single letter or number. It can help you improve over the course of your college career and do your best. . . . You also have the opportunity to write your perspective in your self-evaluation. Reflect on why you chose this offering, what you hoped to learn, and what you experienced along the way. . . . People who read your transcript will get a full picture of what you did in college and what your work ethic is like. Graduate schools appreciate the level of detail, because it shows the depth of work. Your evaluations can demonstrate how prepared you are for graduate-level study. ("Narrative Evaluations" 2019)

When parents, board members, and legislators realize that narrative evaluation isn't simply the latest fad in education, but one that highly respected colleges and universities have been using for decades, they often become far more willing to give this technique a chance. In addition, the proof that institutions like New College of Florida and The Evergreen State College can provide that employers and other schools recognize the value of narrative evaluation and that it doesn't hinder the success of students later in life can paint a very compelling picture.

FURTHER IDEAS TO IMPROVE STUDENT EVALUATION

The education policy researcher, Gerald Bracey (1940–2009), was a strong and vocal critic of standardized testing who argued that the types of tests mandated in schools were worthless at assessing some of the most important capacities students needs to develop, including "creativity, critical thinking, resilience, motivation, persistence, curiosity, endurance, reliability, enthusiasm, empathy, self-awareness, self-discipline, leadership, civic-mindedness, courage, compassion, resourcefulness, sense of beauty, sense of wonder, honesty, [and] integrity" (Harris, Smith, and Harris 2011, p. 25). Fortunately, however, those capacities *can* be appraised and improved through the use of narrative evaluation.

One way in which school leaders can make narrative evaluation even more valuable is to choose a subset of capacities from Bracey's list— narrowed perhaps by grade level, subject area, or the school's mission and values—and encourage teachers to address these capacities whenever appropriate in their narrative evaluations. Prompts can even be included in the templates that teachers develop as a way of making sure that these aspects of personal growth are not excluded from their evaluations. Examples of such prompts include the following:

- With regard to creativity, [NAME] has demonstrated that s/he [CITE ONE SPECIFIC ACHIEVEMENT OR CHALLENGE WITH REGARD TO CREATIVITY].
- [NAME] is [HIGHLY SUCCESSFUL/OFTEN SUCCESSFUL/SOME-WHAT CHALLENGED/REGULARLY CHALLENGED] at self-motivation and, in the future, should be encouraged to [STATE SPECIFIC RECOMMENDATION].
- [NAME] is a/n [DESCRIPTIVE TERM] leader who [IS ROUTINELY RELIED ON BY OTHER STUDENTS/BUILDS TEAMS WELL/ CREATES CONFLICT WHERE IT IS NOT ALWAYS NECESSARY/ HAS DIFFICULTY FOLLOWING THROUGH ON DECISIONS/TOO OFTEN WORKS ALONE RATHER THAN COLLABORATIVELY].
- In terms of integrity, [NAME] [MAINTAINS THE HIGHEST STANDARDS OF PERSONAL CONDUCT/IS SOMETIMES WILLING TO CUT CORNERS IN ORDER TO ACHIEVE A GOAL/HAS ENGAGED IN QUESTIONABLE BEHAVIORS THAT NEED TO BE ADDRESSED].

In addition, as teachers become more proficient at developing narrative evaluations that flow seamlessly from their learning objectives, they help students develop in two areas simultaneously: process and progress.

For the process criteria, they evaluate their students on effort, work habits, and the manner with which they arrive at conclusions. For the progress criteria, they appraise how much knowledge students have acquired from their learning experiences, how far they have advanced academically, and which areas remain as challenges to continued growth. This approach allows for a more personalized learning environment and allows the school to move beyond evaluating only the type of learning that can be reflected in multiple-choice tests and labeled by either a letter grade or numerical score.

As has been stated repeatedly, *it is not necessary to abandon traditional grades and scores entirely in order to incorporate narrative evaluation into a school's standard procedures*. But, as a way of complementing traditional approaches, narrative assessments help students learn how to reflect, grow, change, and adapt.

They make students *self-regulated learners* with the ability to plan for tasks, monitor their own performance, reflect on the outcome, and then do even better next time. In short, they produce students who can continue to be their own teachers long after they complete their last exams and receive their final diplomas.

A CASE STUDY ON EFFECTIVE STUDENT EVALUATION

Imagine that you are about to write a narrative evaluation about a math unit for a second-grade student, Missy Sippy, that you'll share with her mother, Mrs. Sippy, at an upcoming parent-teacher conference. Here's what you've observed about Missy's performance:

- Missy has been struggling with the concepts discussed in class. She gives up easily when encountering a challenging problem and doesn't have confidence in her abilities even though she actually understands more than she thinks.
- She has been making more progress lately, however, in the areas of persisting even when initially confused and in identifying the specific concepts that she does not yet understand.
- Of her math skills, the ability to do simple arithmetic (add, subtract, and multiply) in her head is currently the strongest.
- Her weakest skill right now is developing strategies for approaching complex story problems.
- When engaged in the project involving her daily study plan, Missy could correctly calculate when different activities should begin, but she was often confused about the concept of elapsed time.
- She tends to make her greatest progress when she's given ample time and allowed to figure out the challenge on her own.
- While rarely a self-starter, Missy is an excellent example for other students on all matters related to integrity and personal honesty.

Based on these observations, write a narrative evaluation of Missy's performance using the template provided earlier for the hypothetical example of Cy Burnett and several of the additional prompts provided in the discussion of Gerald Bracey's list of desirable capacities in students.

DISCUSSION OF THE CASE STUDY

The precise evaluation that you write will depend on your own writing style and matters of personal preference, but one possible narrative evaluation for Missy Sippy might look like the following:

> Missy Sippy is an emerging mathematician. She continues to demonstrate great strength in the area of mental calculations and is now making progress in developing greater confidence in her abilities. Missy has grown in identifying the specific concepts that she does not yet understand. While solving complex story problems remains an area that she finds challenging, Missy is improving in her time-telling skills. The concept of elapsed time does remain a challenge,

though. Her progress to date suggests, however, that this skill will improve with further work in this area. During the project involving elapsed time skills and the students' daily plans, she was able appropriately to calculate when different activities should begin. Her application of skills through performance demonstrates that she should be assigned additional problem sets to work on her own at her own speed and not rushed. In the next unit, Missy will be encouraged to incorporate additional work on elapsed time into the new material that students will encounter. Missy is somewhat challenged at self-motivation and, in the future, should be encouraged to set priorities and pursue them without external prompting by the teacher. In terms of integrity, Missy maintains the highest standards of personal conduct and is an excellent example for other students on all matters related to integrity and personal honesty.

KEY POINTS IN THIS CHAPTER

- While standardized tests are required in schools, the research suggests that they are actually rather poor methods for determining what students have learned.
- In a similar way, letter grades and numerical scores may not provide much information about exactly what a student has mastered and what still remains a challenge.
- Assigning letter grades and numerical scores often causes students to focus solely on the result, not on the process that led to that result. They thus tend to identify themselves as "good at" this subject or "bad at" that subject without really understanding how they can improve.
- Incorporating at least some narrative evaluation into a school's strategies for appraising student work can avoid many of these problems.
- Narrative evaluation helps prepare students for the workforce since it is the type of performance appraisal commonly used in many work environments.
- Several highly selective colleges and universities also use narrative evaluation, sometimes as a complete replacement for numerical scores and letter grades. Their experience suggests that narrative evaluations do not become obstacles for the students' admission to further schooling or to being hired as an employee.
- In order to perform narrative evaluation effectively, teachers often need special training and additional time (at least initially) to engage in the process.
- The use of templates can reduce the amount of time needed for narrative evaluation.
- Narrative evaluation helps teachers provide guidance in important areas of student performance that are difficult to quantify, such as creativity, leadership, and personal integrity.

REFERENCES

Harris, P., B. M. Smith, & J. Harris. 2011. *The Myths of Standardized Tests: Why They Don't Tell You What You Think They Do*. Lanham, MD: Rowman & Littlefield.

"Narrative Evaluations." 2019. The Evergreen State College. https://www.evergreen.edu/evaluations

"Narrative Method For Tracking and Documenting Employee Contributions." 2018. Performance Resource Center. http://performance-appraisals.org/Bacalsappraisalarticles/articles/narratives1.htm

Schwartz, K. 2018. "A Grading Strategy That Puts the Focus on Learning from Mistakes." https://www.kqed.org/mindshift/52456/a-grading-strategy-that-puts-the-focus-on-learning-from-mistakes.

"We're Different By Design." 2019. New College of Florida. https://www.ncf.edu/academics/academics-at-new-college/

RESOURCES

Andrade, H. L., & M. Heritage. 2017. *Using Formative Assessment to Enhance Learning, Achievement, and Academic Self-regulation*. New York, NY: Routledge.

Kohn, A. 2000. *The Case Against Standardized Testing: Raising the Scores, Ruining the Schools*. Portsmouth, NH: Heineman.

Meier, D., & M. Knoester. 2017. *Beyond Testing: Seven Assessments of Students and Schools More Effective Than Standardized Tests*. New York, NY: Teachers College Press.

Nilson, L. B. 2013. *Creating Self-Regulated Learners: Strategies to Strengthen Students' Self-awareness and Learning Skills*. Sterling, VA: Stylus.

Nilson, L. B. 2015. *Specifications Grading: Restoring Rigor, Motivating Students, and Saving Faculty Time*. Sterling, VA: Stylus.

Schneider, M. C., & R. L. Johnson. 2017. *Using Student Learning Objectives for Assessment*. New York, NY: Routledge.

Chapter Eight

Disengaged and Overly Engaged Parents

Helicopter parents. Even though this expression has only been around since 1990 (Cline and Fay 1990, pp. 23–24), you only have to utter these words for everyone in the room to understand exactly what you mean: those overly engaged and protective parents who always seem to be hovering over their children like helicopters, never allowing them to become fully independent and always eager to defend them from all foes, real or imagined.

In fact, if you attend professional meetings that deal with parent/teacher relations, you'll find that this original coinage has been joined by a host of (sometimes clever, sometimes offensive) expressions, including the following:

- *Stealth bomber or SEAL Team Six parents* who seem to "swoop in" out of nowhere and leave a trail of destruction in their wake.
- *Blackhawk parents* who show up "with guns blazing," demand immediate action, and won't wait to learn about other sides of the issue.
- *Drone parents* who know all of their children's passwords and quietly observe all of their communications and media postings, including notices from teachers and school leaders. Drone parents sometimes even pretend to be their children in online forums in an attempt to gather information about teachers and administrators or request special consideration.
- *Snowplow or bulldozer parents* who try to push aside every obstacle or inconvenience for their children.
- *Hotline parents* who immediately contact the principal or superintendent whenever they feel their children have been undervalued, challenged, or offended in some way. (Rosenblum 2016; Taylor 2006; Buller 2009; Lamberson 2007; Shellenbarger 2007; Howe n.d.)

As aggravating as these overly involved, too-attached parents can be, an even greater problem in many schools are the parents who aren't nearly engaged enough. These *absentee landlord parents*, as they might be called, are often depicted as taking little or no responsibility for their children's behavior or academic development.

They're regarded by many as assuming that rearing their children is the school's job, not their own, and finding fault with teachers and administrators when their children perform poorly or engage in activities that harm themselves or others. Although there are many completely understandable reasons why parents may appear to be disengaged in their children's education, as we'll see later, it can be easy for teachers to assume that absentee landlord parents simply don't care.

To be sure, the vast majority of parents don't fit either of these patterns. They want to be involved in their children's development, of course, but they also understand that development sometimes means letting students make their own mistakes. They're eager to partner with the schools, not to see them as either adversaries or daycare centers. But what should you do when you're faced with parents who do lose track of the proper level of involvement with the school? How do you deal with parents who become engaged in their children's education far too much or far too little?

OPTIMAL PARENTAL INVOLVEMENT

In the best possible situation, teachers and parents work together harmoniously as a team in order to foster the education and development of students. Parents can reinforce the importance of what goes on at school, and teachers can support the sort of personal development that goes on at home. When behavioral challenges occur in school, parents can work productively with teachers to encourage students to apply themselves more completely to their studies, interact respectfully with others, and act responsibly with regard to school facilities and equipment.

Open discussion about the school's mission, culture, and values is a school leader's best strategy in trying to achieve this optimal level of parental involvement. When parents know that they and the school's staff "are on the same page" with regard to helping students achieve, they are much more likely to be cooperative and supportive. In their book on how to create meaningful student partnerships, the authors of *Beyond the Bake Sale* (2007) describe the situation this way:

> Parents have told us that they are more likely to be angry and lose control when they feel no one cares about their situation or will listen to them. Many—but not all—problems can be prevented by developing trusting rela-

tionships that welcome and honor families. (Henderson, Mapp, Johnson, and Davies 2007, p. 152)

Moreover, when parents understand that a school's mission includes goals that they can be excited about—such as leadership development, the encouragement of creativity, entrepreneurialism, civic engagement, critical thinking, and the like—they tend to echo in the home the same message that their children are receiving in school.

Frequent communication with parents can reduce the likelihood that disengagement and excessive engagement will be a widespread problem at the school. Potential disengaged parents will learn about exciting activities in which they can become involved even if their schedules are already filled with numerous demands. Potential overly engaged parents will be more at ease in letting teachers and administrators do their jobs because they'll know exactly what the school will do for their children, what the expectations are, and how they can participate in constructive ways to further the school's mission.

But what should school leaders do when this optimal situation doesn't occur? How do they deal effectively with helicopter parents, absentee landlords, or any other type of parent whose actions are not in the best interests of their children? These are difficult questions, and they go to the heart of the issue of a parent's rights to bring up his or her children in whatever way that parent sees fit.

Certainly, no one would argue that schools should be able to interfere with how parents choose to rear their children. Nevertheless, teachers and school leaders also have a responsibility to look out for the interests of their students and to try to create the best learning environment they can. Since the strategies used to deal with overly engaged and disengaged parents are different, it's best to address them separately, beginning with the issue of what school leaders should do when confronted by helicopter parents and the like.

LISTEN TO THE MESSAGE BEHIND THE MESSAGE

It may as well be admitted: overly engaged parents can be annoying and disruptive to the mission of educating *all* the students of a school. Because they can be irritants, they are often dismissed by teachers and school leaders, or an attempt is made to marginalize them in some way. But doing so can cause you to overlook a crucial question. If parents feel a need to become so involved in their children's lives that they can't even let go for the duration of a school day, why are they doing so? What has given rise to their concern that the needs and interests of their children will not be met unless they intervene aggressively on the students' behalf?

If parents are truly treated as equal partners in the educational process, they can provide valuable insights that enable teachers and administrators to do their job better. They can explain why a student may be unable to focus on his or her schoolwork, acts inappropriately in certain settings, or interacts poorly with others.

You may not learn everything you need to know in a single conversation. Parents may initially be defensive when they feel that their children are being accused of poor behavior or lack of academic progress. An extended series of conversations may be necessary before they realize that their voices are truly being heard and their concerns taken seriously.

If the overt message that overly engaged parents often give is, "I have to act as my child's advocate because no one else is doing so," the truly important message is one level deeper. What, if anything, did members of the school community do to give the parents the impression that the needs of their children are not being properly addressed? As Brian Gatens, the superintendent of Emerson School District in New Jersey, notes,

> My experience has been that an overparenting family is acting primarily out of a genuine fear that their child may struggle academically or miss out on future academic opportunities. . . . Understanding the behavior doesn't excuse it. You just need to take certain steps for your peace of mind and the long-term needs of the child. (Gatens 2015)

There's often a misconception, fed by the media and popular entertainment, that a child will never be accepted into a top-ranked college or university if that child has anything less than a stellar record from preschool onward. There is also a corollary misconception that a lifetime of success is only available to those who attend a top-ranked college or university (or indeed any college or university at all instead of other postsecondary opportunities for career development). By listening compassionately to the concerns of parents and then providing accurate information that will help to counteract these misconceptions, school leaders can go a long way toward reducing the worst excesses of overly engaged parents.

If it turns out that the parent does have a legitimate concern because of a child's particular need, you can describe the resources that the school has available. As was outlined in chapter 6, an individualized education program (IEP; a plan that follows policies developed by the Department of Education and that addresses only educational work through the twelfth grade) or a 504 plan (a plan that follows policies developed by the Office of Civil Rights and that addresses accommodations that may be necessary in school, employment, and college) can help ensure that all the child's needs are being met. Because these programs are mandated by federal law, you can help relieve the parent's anxieties about how seriously the school will treat these plans.

REMEMBER THAT EDUCATION REQUIRES DEVELOPING INDEPENDENCE OF THOUGHT

One of the first things taught in many undergraduate programs in education is the origin of the word *education* itself. The term is derived from the Latin prefix *e-* meaning *out of* and the verb *ducere* meaning *to lead.* As Muriel Sparks's fictional teacher Miss Jean Brodie says,

> To me education is a leading out of what is already there in the pupil's soul. To Miss Mackay it is a putting in of something that is not there, and that is not what I call education. I call it intrusion. (Sparks 2018, p. 36)

What education "leads out" of the student is independence of thought and action, with the result that overly engaged parents sometimes, unintentionally and for perfectly admirable reasons, end up interfering with the very educational process they think they're trying to support.

With that independence comes responsibility, and that level of responsibility increases according to a child's age. By communicating the important role that the development of responsibility and independence of thought has in your school's mission, you have a constructive way of helping parents understand that it's perfectly appropriate for children to find their own way in difficult situations, even if it causes some temporary discomfort.

No one learns how to ride a bicycle properly until the training wheels come off, and, as one learns, an occasional fall may occur. That's only to be expected; it's part of the process. And that process can't take place if the parents always intervene to "put the training wheels back on" whenever things become temporarily "unsteady."

In the words of Brian Gatens, "It's essential that children develop the ability to speak to an adult about a question or a concern. This type of self-advocacy will serve them well when they're no longer under the direct supervision of their parents" (Gatens 2015). It is sometimes difficult for overly engaged parents to understand that, in their well-meaning attempts to protect their children, they're also interfering with their children's ability to grow in responsibility, self-advocacy, and independent problem solving. As challenging as it may be to convey that message to parents, doing so with compassion and diplomacy will be necessary at times.

SEE THE ISSUE FROM THE STUDENT'S PERSPECTIVE

As another means of fostering independence in the student, it can be useful to talk to the child and try to understand how he or she sees the underlying issue that is causing the parent's interference. At times, the student will be even more frustrated than teachers and administrators that the parent is always hovering nearby and unwilling to let the child speak with his or her own voice.

You may gain insights into the reasons for the parent's behavior, such as the student's struggles with anxiety, bullying, or lack of self-esteem. By using the school's resources to address these underlying issues, you eliminate the *need* for the parent to be overly involved and may even gain the parent's trust that you do indeed have the child's best interests at heart.

CREATE APPROPRIATE OUTLETS FOR PARENTAL INVOLVEMENT

Parents sometimes interfere inappropriately with what schools are trying to accomplish because they're unaware of how they can become more active *appropriately*. The most readily apparent avenue for constructive parent involvement is your school's parent-teacher organization, but there are also other options available. As the National Education Association says on its website,

> The overly involved helicopter parent can be aggressive, but put a group of them together and re-channel their energy—into study groups for their gifted children, for example—and you've provided a positive outlet for their Type A traits. Some of the most heavily involved parents are driven and successful in their fields. Take advantage of that drive and tap into their expertise . . . Invite a parent with a legal career to talk to classes about the Constitution and government. (National Education Association 2007)

Treating parents as the experts they are can help transform adversaries into resources. It demonstrates respect for the contributions they can make to the students' education and thus often elicits respect for the contributions *you* make.

Redirecting the negative involvement of overly engaged parents into more positive channels can also be accomplished by encouraging the parents to take a leadership role in fundraising activities, booster clubs, lobbying efforts, and community outreach.

Parents sometimes become overly involved in what the school is doing because, after years of feeling as though they were the most important people in their children's lives, they've now lost that role. You can restore that sense of importance and involvement by helping them discover a new role, one that further advances a goal vital to your school's mission.

RESPOND ONLY IN APPROPRIATE AND PROFESSIONAL WAYS

There are times when overly involved parents cross the line from being mere irritants to becoming serious impediments to the educational work of the school. When that occurs, it can be tempting for teachers and administrators to feel that their patience has been exhausted and to respond with anger and exasperation. Doing so is almost always counterproductive. It confirms the parents' suspicion that they and the school are not "on the same side" and may irreparably break any trust in your good intentions that still remains.

Taking a stance that appears to helicopter parents to be adversarial is often one of the worst things you can do. It heightens tensions rather than eases them. The parents approach these situations believing that they have a valid concern that's being overlooked.

They're not really saying that the teachers are ineffective and that the administration is incompetent, although that's often how it feels when you're on the receiving end of their remarks. They may simply treat everyone rudely. As one observer says,

> Some people are just abrasive, argumentative, or difficult. They are like this with the person at the deli counter, with the person at the post office, and with people they work with. They may even be like that with family members. It stands to reason, then that they would not deviate from this approach dealing with teachers or school leaders. (Clouducation 2012)

If you take an aggressive response, the parents receive the impression that you're belittling their concerns and arguing that, when it comes to rearing children, you have far more expertise than they. The exchange then becomes mired in mutual accusations (or implied accusations) of failure, rather than moving to more productive ground.

Sarah Fudin, who writes a blog on pedagogical matters for the University of Southern California's Rossier School of Education, offers the following advice: "Be empathetic and put yourself in the parent's shoes. Be a good listener and breathe. . . . The worst thing that you can do is react poorly and put a permanent strain on the relationship" (Fudin 2012). Speak to the parents as you would want someone to speak to you if that person believed, rightly or wrongly, that you had overstepped your bounds. Demonstrate the same compassion and support that you would show any other member of the school community who has a concern.

Parents become overly engaged because they care deeply about their children's welfare. In that way, teachers, administrators, staff members, and parents all have something in common: all of them want to protect the child's best interests. Whenever communication seems strained or antagonistic, therefore, try to keep that shared goal in mind. Validate the parents' *feelings* even if you can't validate the specific actions they are demanding. Remember at all times that, if the parents did not care at least as much as you do, they wouldn't be there having this conversation with you.

Whenever possible, conduct the conversation in a space that puts the parents at rest. Take a walk together. If school is not in session, identify whichever environment at the school seems most calming and suggest that the conversation take place there. Listen carefully without interrupting, jot down an occasional note if there are actions you'll need to follow up on later, and try not to sound as anxious or angry as you may actually be feeling.

ESTABLISH BOUNDARIES THAT ARE IN THE INTEREST OF EVERYONE CONCERNED

Setting boundaries with overly engaged parents doesn't mean shutting them out of the school involvement entirely or making yourself incommunicado. It means making it clear when and where visits from parents are appropriate and which issues are strictly within the school's domain of responsibility.

Parents who are making a presentation to the school or assisting in some other way should be given both a starting and an ending time for their activities. Parents who are coming by for discussions should be scheduled late in the afternoon when they're less likely to interfere with the other responsibilities of teachers and administrators during the workday.

Requiring teachers to post grading scales and rubrics is not only good pedagogy, but it's also a way of setting a boundary when a parent tries to have a student's grade changed. By having the standards by which the grades will be assigned outlined clearly and objectively, it becomes easier to explain to a very insistent parent why an assignment or test received a particular score and why it wouldn't be appropriate or fair to the other students to change it.

Another way of setting boundaries is making sure that all professional communications are kept separate from personal communications. Almost everyone who works at a school these days has a professional email address that is shared with parents and students and a personal email address that is used only with friends and family.

But that same approach can be used with personal and professional cell phones. A teacher or administrator can then set a policy of never answering his or her professional cell phone except during certain hours of the day. It may even be a good idea to leave these cell phones at school and never take them home. As long as there is a specified number that students and parents can call in an actual emergency, this policy protects teachers and leaders from being constantly on call.

Many schools have also adopted the policy of making certain types of email communication one-way. In other words, their system allows announcements to be sent to students and parents but does not allow the recipient merely to click on reply (or worse, reply all) and respond to the announcement. If your school does not have this capability, you might consider using a service like Mail-List.com, remind.com, ClassParrot, or ClassPager, which allow text messages or emails to be sent without the ability for the recipient to respond.

Once again, the point of these restrictions is not to isolate the school from its stakeholders but merely to set time, place, and manner restrictions on when nonemergency communication can be made. As the poet Robert Frost famously said, "Good fences make good neighbors." In a similar way, we might add that appropriate boundaries make for appropriate parent-teacher relations.

KEEP THOROUGH RECORDS

Keeping good notes on interactions with overly engaged parents is useful in case there are disagreements later about what agreements were made, whether follow-up actions occurred, how many contacts the parents made with the school, and similar matters. Your school may even require that documentation be maintained on all contacts with parents. Even if that policy doesn't exist, your own records on what was discussed and when may be invaluable if parents ever contact the superintendent or school board, alleging that your school hasn't been attentive to the needs of their children.

DEALING WITH DISENGAGED PARENTS

Although it can be frustrating to deal with parents who can't grant their children any independence even for the duration of a school day, an even more common (and troubling) occurrence is parents who seem not to care at all about their children's education. When a child of disengaged parents has a behavioral problem, the parents are often unwilling to become partners with the school in addressing the issue. They attend school events rarely, miss or resent coming to parent-teacher conferences, and see little if any overlap between their goals as parents and teachers' jobs as educators.

In a famous series of research that began in the 1950s and extended over several decades, the developmental psychologist Diana Baumrind (1927–2018) identified a number of what she called "parenting styles." While Baumrind's precise system of categorization evolved over time, her original description of what she termed unengaged or disengaged parents was that they tended to be "neither demanding nor responsive. . . . They do not structure or monitor. In addition, it was found that unengaged mothers were nonagentic (i.e., they tended not to be proactive, self-reflective, or self-regulating), families were disorganized with 60% divorced, and both parents manifested problem behavior" (Baumrind 1991, pp. 65).

In addition, as the educational consultant Kendra Cherry summarizes Baumrind's characterization,

> Uninvolved parents make few to no demands of their children and they are often indifferent, dismissive, or even completely neglectful. . . . These parents have little emotional involvement with their kids. While they provide for basic needs like food and shelter, they are, for the most part, uninvolved in their children's lives. . . .

- They're emotionally distant from their children.
- They offer little or no supervision.
- They show little warmth, love, and affection towards their children.
- They have few or no expectations or demands for behavior.
- They don't attend school events and parent-teacher conferences.
- They may intentionally avoid their children.

> They're often too overwhelmed by their own problems to deal with their children. (Cherry 2018)

Nevertheless, that image of parental disengagement appears to be fairly narrow. While there are undoubtedly parents who are apathetic, disorganized, and prone to problem behavior, the vast majority of disengaged parents in contemporary society don't fit this mold.

For example, the British training website for school leaders, Creative Education, lists ten common reasons for parents to be less engaged in school activities than teachers and administrators may want them to be.

1. They may have their own unpleasant memories of being in school and feel that being asked to come to the school is more similar to being sent to the principal's office than being invited to a party.
2. Their children may discourage them from "making a fuss" because it embarrasses them.
3. They may believe that it's only appropriate for them to get involved when there's a problem.
4. There may be such infrequent communication from the school that they don't believe a genuine dialogue exists.
5. Their work schedule may not allow them to be present at the school when school leaders wish them to be.
6. They may be intimidated by their own lack of education and believe that it's best to leave teaching to qualified teachers.

7. They may feel that they don't have enough information about their children's educational progress to understand how they could help.
8. There may be a language barrier. In a multicultural society, some parents may not be fluent in the language of the majority population.
9. They may believe that too many teachers speak in educational jargon and "psychobabble" that they don't understand.
10. They may find the traditional ways in which parent evenings are structured to be boring or unpleasant. (Creative Education n.d.)

The fact of the matter is that the society in which schools operate today is complex, diverse, and very different from that which existed when Diana Baumrind began her study. In addition, some parents may not be as engaged in their children's education as they would like to be due to illness, single parenthood, poverty, or other extenuating circumstances. Different expectations parents have of schools due to culture may play a role as well.

As a result, it's both unfair and highly unproductive to approach the challenge of parental engagement with the assumption that disengaged parents are simply lazy, don't care, or are callously toxic to their children's development. If school leaders want to increase the likelihood that parents will join with them as true partners in their children's educations, they must

- provide multiple ways for parents to engage with students and their schools: virtually, in person, simultaneously, asynchronously, and in any other manner that fits contemporary work schedules and lifestyles.
- conduct two-way communication with parents in terms they can understand, jargon-free, and in a language that is comfortable for them.
- communicate the message that school today isn't the same as when the parents were students themselves and that they should find interactions with teachers and administrators to be open, pleasant, and nonthreatening.
- understand what parents find pleasant and unpleasant about open house events and other formal school activities in order to make these opportunities better structured to suit the needs and interests of parents.
- make absolutely certain that the only time parents hear from schools isn't when their children are sick or in trouble or when the schools want something from the parents.

Brian Gatens, whose advice about dealing with overly engaged parents was presented earlier, also offers some useful insights about how to deal with parents who initially act as though they're disengaged. He notes that school leaders should embrace any willingness of the parent to help his or her child to succeed as an important first step on what should be an ongoing process.

In a perfect world, a parent would check every homework assignment every night, quiz her child and help her prepare projects and assignments. The disengaged parent needs a more realistic start, like sitting down with her child every night and reviewing the homework pad or checking the school website together. Perhaps even the simple goal of side-by-side reading or a nightly "quiet time" to study is a good place to start. (Gatens 2012)

Teachers and administrators have to understand the pressures that are on parents these days. To many adults today, it can feel as though their doctors want them to spend all their time focusing on their health, their dentists want them to spend all their time focusing on their teeth, their mechanics want them to spend all their time focusing on their cars, their bosses want them to spend all their time focusing on their jobs, and their children's teachers want them to spend all their time focusing on their children's education.

The result is a feeling many people have that they aren't living up to the expectations of others in any aspect of their lives. They're not really disengaged parents; they're just overwhelmed.

The school leader's goal should be to help parents understand that they're not alone in the challenges they face. Faculty and staff at the school will be vigilant in applying the highest level of professional skill in helping all students succeed. The school isn't asking for parents to be full-time educators in addition to all their other responsibilities. It's offering its partnership to help the parents achieve a goal that the teachers and administrators share: giving their children every opportunity to live the best life possible.

A CASE STUDY IN DEALING WITH DISENGAGED AND OVERLY ENGAGED PARENTS

Maxie and Minnie Mumm have a daughter, Chrysantha, who attends Absentee Helicopter Elementary School in Oxymoron, a small town located not far from where you are right now. Maxie and Minnie are devoted to one another, although they have dramatically different approaches when it comes to Chrysantha's education.

Maxie is definitely a "hands-on" parent. He runs his consulting business from his home, which is located less than five minutes away from the school, and drops Chrysantha off each morning and picks her up each afternoon. The principal of Absentee Helicopter Elementary, Dr. Anita Break, can't recall a day when Maxie hasn't stopped by at least once, usually to offer a piece of advice on how the school could be run better or to point out the inadequacies of one of Chrysantha's teachers.

Maxie knows the name of each student in Chrysantha's class and tries to help Anita by letting her know which students she should let Chrysantha hang around with and which students she should keep Chrysantha away from. He also likes to "correct the corrections" (as he calls it) on his daughter's assignments and exams, noting why Chrysantha's answer was always better than what the teacher had suggested. If Maxie doesn't receive satisfaction in having the grade changed at the school level, he has a habit of appealing the matter to the superintendent and school board.

Lately, because a number of school shootings have been reported on the news, Maxie has become a vocal advocate of increased school safety measures. Although students and all visitors must pass through metal detectors when entering the building, Maxie has questioned why Anita hasn't taken "more of a TSA approach," with officers on site to inspect individually every bag brought into the building and students required to have their shoes and other possessions X-rayed to make sure dangerous items aren't concealed in them.

Maxie also was the only parent who refused to sign a permission slip allowing Chrysantha to participate in a field trip to the Placidville Art Museum because "big cities like that have high levels of crime, and who knows whether the bus could be in an accident along the way?" As a result, Chrysantha participated in a supervised study hall all day while the other children in the school visited the museum's traveling exhibit of artwork from Walt Disney and Harry Potter movies.

Minnie, on the other hand, has never been seen at the school. She allows Maxie to attend all teacher conferences and parents' night events on his own. Her job as a medical supply company representative keeps her on the road for many days a year. Even when she's home, she must often entertain clients in the evening and complete reports relating to her sales calls. Once when Anita ran into Minnie at the grocery store, she asked Minnie whether Chrysantha was over her cold yet. Minnie said she didn't even know that Chrysantha had had a cold and didn't seem all that concerned by it.

Rasch Judgment, one of Anita's vice principals, believes that Minnie "is just your typical uninvolved parent. She's obviously very emotionally distant from Chrysantha (and I'll bet from Maxie as well). When it comes to parenting, she's just phoning it in—probably like she just phones in her work, too. We can try to fix her, but there's just no getting to some people. If I were you, I'd call her in, refuse to take no for an answer, and make it clear what our expectations are. In fact, I think a little parental audit could do both Minnie and Maxie some good. They're both just enabling Chrysantha in their own way, and we all know where that could lead."

Anita's not sure she agrees with Rasch's assessment of the situation, but she does wish that Maxie were a bit more hands-off and that Minnie were a bit more hands-on. Should she do something, or is it a parental prerogative to engage with the school however much the parent wants? If Anita doesn't do anything, is Rasch right that Chrysantha may suffer from her parents' approaches? If Anita does do something, what should she do?

DISCUSSION OF THE CASE STUDY

A critical question asked at the end of this case study is, "Is it a parental prerogative to engage with the school however much the parent wants?" No matter how frustrating it can be to deal with disengaged and overly engaged parents, it should never be forgotten that the answer to this question is always yes.

None of us has the right to dictate to parents the way in which they should rear their children, even with regard to how often they interact with the school. If school leaders have genuine concerns about a child's safety or welfare, there are appropriate venues for reporting those concerns. But parental involvement with the school rarely crosses over into the realm of child endangerment. There are reasons why, in our best professional judgment, we may wish that a given parent were more or less engaged with the school, but we can never compel them to change their levels of interaction.

With that proviso in mind, however, we may be justified in concluding that Maxie and Minnie Mumm represent clear examples of the overly engaged and the disengaged parent respectively. Maxie appears to be causing Chrysantha to miss out on what could be important opportunities for cultural and social development, such as the field trip to the art museum, by being overly protective and obsessed with her safety beyond a reasonable level.

He may be depriving her of a chance to grow intellectually by repeatedly challenging any correction teachers make to her work. He is diverting the school's principal, superintendent, and board from other work they could be doing to enhance Chrysantha's education by forcing them to address his numerous complaints.

One positive course of action that Anita Break might pursue is to divert Maxie's desire for frequent involvement from forms of interference to forms of collaboration. For example, he could be asked to serve as a parent-chaperone on field trips involving Chrysantha so that he can feel more secure about her safety. He can become active in the school's mission by serving as a *room parent*, in which capacity he could organize class parties around a specific topic that the students were studying, engage in fundraising for special events, send out reminders to other parents about important deadlines, and help the school maintain its contact list of parental information.

Anita could try to listen less to Maxie's overt message ("the school isn't doing its job effectively, and only I can protect Chrysantha") and comprehend the underlying reasons for that message ("I have difficulty letting Chrysantha go and suffer the consequences when she doesn't succeed"). By so doing, she may better understand what Maxie is really afraid of that causes him to act in less than fully productive ways.

Minnie's case, on the other hand, seems to result from the not uncommon challenges of the modern worker with a demanding job. She travels a lot, and, even when she's not on the road, her professional duties frequently occupy almost all her waking hours.

The recommendation by Rasch Judgement that Anita essentially force Maxie to submit to a parental audit is thus likely to be counterproductive. It would probably cause there to be greater barriers between Minnie and the school, and she would be even less inclined to become actively involved in Chrysantha's formal education.

A better course of action, therefore, might be for Anita to start small and build up gradually. Creating opportunities for Minnie to engage with the school electronically and on her own schedule (even if that means posting a quick note online at 2:00 a.m.) could be the beginning of greater parental involvement.

Minnie would learn that serving as an officer of the parent teacher organization and attending long open house events are not the only ways in which she can become engaged. In today's highly connected world, virtual parental involvement is still better than no parental involvement at all.

KEY POINTS IN THIS CHAPTER

- The optimal level of parental involvement with the school begins with an open discussion with all stakeholders about the school's mission, culture, and values.
- School leaders should always remember that overly engaged parents are acting as they do out of genuine love and concern for their children. In the majority of cases, they are not "hovering" because they believe that the staff of the school is incompetent but because they believe that one of their children's critical needs won't be addressed without their advocacy.
- If the current structure of your parent-teacher organization isn't providing sufficient outlets for parental involvement, be creative in identifying other ways for parents to engage productively with the school.
- Although it can require great patience, confrontational encounters with overly engaged parents should always be conducted with restraint, compassion, respect, and empathy.
- Establishing appropriate boundaries with parents does not mean isolating teachers and administrators from their external stakeholders.
- An effective paper trail is always a school leader's best defense if accused of inattentive or improper response to a legitimate parental concern.
- Disengaged parents are usually not unconcerned about their children's education; they are more likely to be overwhelmed by other responsibilities or to feel intimidated by the prospect of interacting with representatives of the school.

- Because of the diversity and complexity of modern society, a variety of means (including the use of technology) should be used to promote optimal parental engagement; not all engagement needs to be conducted in person.

REFERENCES

Baumrind, D. 1991. "The Influence of Parenting Style on Adolescent Competence and Substance Use." *Journal of Early Adolescence 11*(1): 56–95.

Buller, J. L. 2009. "The Excessively Demanding Parent." *Student Affairs Leader 37*(9): 4–5.

Cherry, K. 2018. "What Is Uninvolved Parenting? Characteristics, Effects, and Causes." *Verywellmind*, December 29, 2018. https://www.verywellmind.com/what-is-uninvolved-parenting-2794958

Cline, F., & J. Fay. 1990. *Parenting with Love and Logic: Teaching Children Responsibility.* Colorado Springs, CO: Piñon Press.

Clouducation. 2012. "10 Best Strategies for Dealing with Difficult Parents." https://clouducation.wordpress.com/2012/05/04/10-best-strategies-for-dealing-with-difficult-parents/

Creative Education. n.d. "Overcoming 10 Common Barriers to Parental Engagement." https://www.creativeeducation.co.uk/blog/parental-engagement/

Fudin, S. 2012. "How to Work with Helicopter Parents." *USC Rossier Online*, July 13, 2012. https://rossieronline.usc.edu/how-to-work-with-helicopter-parents/

Gatens, B. 2012. "Disengaged Parents: 5 Keys for School Leaders." *Room 241*, December 19, 2012. https://education.cu-portland.edu/blog/curriculum-teaching-strategies/disengaged-parents-5-keys-for-school-leaders/

Gatens, B. 2015. "Helicopter Parents: How Teachers Can Bring Them Back Down to Earth." *Room 241*, July 15, 2013. https://education.cu-portland.edu/blog/classroom-resources/helicopter-parents-teachers/

Henderson, A. T., K. L. Mapp, V. R. Johnson, & D. Davies. 2007. *Beyond the Bake Sale: The Essential Guide to Family-School Partnerships.* New York, NY: The New Press.

Howe, N. n.d. "Meet Mr. and Mrs. Gen X: A New Parent Generation." *AASA: The School Superintendents Association.* http://www.aasa.org/SchoolAdministratorArticle.aspx?id=11122

Lamberson, J. 2007. "To Parents, Don't Worry, Be Happy." *Daily Illini*, May 26, 2007. https://dailyillini.com/news/2007/05/26/column-to-parents-dont-worry-be-happy/

National Education Association. 2007. "The 'Helicopter Parent.'" http://www.nea.org/archive/16289.htm

Rosenblum, G. 2016. "Helicopter Parents Face off Against Stealth Bombers, Mowers and Drones." *Minnesota Star Tribune*, June 29, 2016. http://www.startribune.com/stealth-bombers-lawn-mowers-and-drones-helicopter-parents-face-competition/384885881/

Shellenbarger, S. 2007. "Helicopter Parenting: A Breakdown." *The Wall Street Journal*, September 27, 2007. https://www.wsj.com/articles/SB119084349844440465

Sparks, M. 2018. *The Prime of Miss Jean Brodie.* New York, NY: Harper Perennial.

Taylor, M. 2006. "Helicopters, Snowplows, and Bulldozers: Managing Students' Parents." *Bulletin of the Association of College Unions International 74*(6): 12–21.

RESOURCES

Constantino, S. M., & P. DeWitt. 2016. *Engage Every Family: Five Simple Principles.* Thousand Oaks, CA: Corwin.

Glass, G. S., & D. Tabatsky. 2014. *The Overparenting Epidemic: Why Helicopter Parenting Is Bad for Your Kids . . . and Dangerous for You, Too!* New York, NY: Skyhorse.

Hong, S., & J. Anyon. 2011. *A Cord of Three Strands: A New Approach to Parent Engagement in Schools.* Cambridge, MA: Harvard Education.

Lightfoot, S. L. 2004. *The Essential Conversation: What Parents and Teachers Can Learn from Each Other.* New York, NY: Random House.

Mapp, K. L., I. Carver, & J. Lander. 2017. *Powerful Partnerships: A Teacher's Guide to Engaging Families for Student Success.* New York, NY: Scholastic.

Whitaker, T., & D. J. Fiore. 2016. *Dealing with Difficult Parents* (2nd ed.). New York, NY: Routledge.

Chapter Nine

External Pressures on Schools and School Leaders

In chapter 7, there was a reference to a maxim familiar to nearly all school leaders, even though it's rarely discussed in courses on educational leadership or in professional development programs: *everyone thinks they know how to run a school simply because they've* been *to school*. As a result, it can sometimes be very difficult to advance your own vision for your school because many of your stakeholders are insistent upon their own visions, which may be difficult to reconcile with what you're convinced is in the best interests of your students and community.

It's not as though these stakeholders actually see themselves as in opposition to you, at least not most of the time. In the vast majority of cases, they're seriously trying to help, but they often base their recommendations on their own experience at school, and that experience may not be typical of the student body you're now serving. They may also be romanticizing their recollections of what it was like to attend school "back in the day," feeling that everything was perfect then even though that is unlikely to have been the case.

EXTERNAL PRESSURES

Each school leader may experience external pressure from different quarters, but the following are some of the most common groups that principals and other administrators may encounter that can be well-intended but sometimes cause frustrating challenges.

Members of the School Board

People usually serve on school boards because they have a sincere interest in educational quality. But interest isn't always accompanied by expertise. They may assume that the way in which they'd solve a problem in their own professions (such as business, the military, or the government) is an effective way to solve a problem in your school, even if that's not the case. Dealing with members of the school board can be challenging because the board, in a very real sense, is your boss, and it's unwise to dismiss their concerns openly or to ignore their advice.

Members of the school board often shift onto school leaders the pressures that they themselves are feeling from parents, legislatures, and special interest groups. Probably the most effective approach you can take is to be diplomatic, listen attentively to their advice, and express appreciation that they shared their perspectives with you.

In many cases, what board members want is to be heard. They want to be able to assure whoever brought the issue to their attention that they have addressed it with you. They're not necessarily expecting an immediate answer or a radical change in policy. What they're expecting is to be taken seriously and treated as though their insights are valuable.

There will, of course, be occasions in which your values and vision for your school are in conflict with the advice you're receiving from your board. In these situations, choose your battles carefully. Not every hill is one worth dying on, and it's appropriate to ask yourself, "Is what I'm doing merely my preferred way of approaching this situation, or is it something that I feel passionate about and that is integral to my school's mission, vision, and values?"

A direct order must be followed, of course. There is, after all, a chain of command that simply can't be ignored. But if implementing a *request* from the board would cause you to lead in a way that's inauthentic or that is likely to cause serious problems for your school, making your strongest case about *why* you can't honor that request is far better than merely flouting or ignoring it.

If what the board is requesting reflects something that you can do, even though you would prefer another course of action or feel that your own plan is only slightly better, then your best plan of action is probably to do what the board member is asking.

Acting in this way will create good will for you and your school and may also help you in those situations when you absolutely cannot act in the way the member asks. You'll be able to remind the person that, in other circumstances, you were more than happy to take his or her advice. But unfortunately, as matters currently stand, you simply cannot honor the request because of the compelling reasons that you outline.

Legislatures

In certain ways, legislatures are like school boards "writ large." They, too, set educational policies, but, unlike boards that serve only a single school or system, they do so for an entire state. School leaders should recognize that, because of the pressures for reelection that legislators are under, the goals of lawmaking bodies may not align perfectly with the goals of the school. Legislators frequently want to see improving metrics, and, as has been suggested repeatedly throughout this book, metrics often don't tell the whole story. In fact, they may tell the *wrong* story.

Since metrics compel schools to assess the assessable and quantify the quantifiable, the students' retention of information tends to be given priority over personal growth, self-discovery, the refinement of leadership skills, and other matters that, although critically important, are difficult to measure through standardized tests.

Legislators may thus encourage schools, openly or implicitly, to reduce the time spent on activities that school leaders and other education professionals regard as important and increase the time spent in class on the information and processes that lead to higher standardized test scores, even if that information and those processes have little long-term value.

Legislatures can also place schools in a challenging double bind. They may want the test scores at a school to increase at the same time that they want teachers to avoid grade inflation. They may acknowledge progress in improving test scores largely by setting even more ambitious goals in the future, resulting in more and more time spent simply teaching to the test.

Legislatures also resemble school boards in creating mandates that school leaders are required to follow. In this way, too, the legislature is your de facto boss. As with any boss, it can be career-ending and counterproductive to resist the legislature openly. You'll have much greater success if you work through appropriate representatives, like the teachers' union and professional groups, in advocating for critical issues with a united front. Write to your legislators. Speak to your legislators. Make a compelling case about what should be done while at the same time respecting the legislature's right to pass laws affecting your school.

The Superintendent

If the legislature is your de facto boss, the superintendent is your *actual* boss, at least if you work at a public school. Like the school board, many superintendents have a tendency to "push downward" onto principals and other school leaders the pressures that they themselves are experiencing from their stakeholders.

That practice can be frustrating since it may mean that you spend a lot of time responding to the superintendent's initiatives rather than following your own vision for the school. On the other hand, the only way in which you can make your vision for the school a reality is to make sure that you have your supervisor's support. So, trade-offs are sometimes inevitable.

As you gain more and more of your superintendent's trust, consider initiating a candid conversation about the advantages of site-based management, an administrative approach in which most authority for day-to-day decisions is delegated to individual schools, decision making is shared among various stakeholder groups, and leaders are empowered in matters of mission, values, and culture at the school level (Levey and Acker-Hocevar 1998).

This approach allows those people who best understand the impact of decisions in their own environments to make those decisions. In the long term, site-based management actually makes your superintendent's job easier. He or she is freer to delegate issues to local school leaders rather than make so many minor decisions that it's not possible to spend time on the truly important decisions.

Members of the school board, legislators, and superintendents all require school leaders to develop skills in *managing up*, the practice of providing the levels above you with what they need so that you can be more effective at providing the levels below you with what those levels need. Effective managing up begins with asking yourself two questions: "What concerns does someone at that level have that I myself do not have?" and "How am I best able to address those concerns while still preserving the degree of autonomy I need in order to be effective?"

School leaders sometimes feel as though they have to support and appease those above them at the same time that they persuade and coax those below them. But in some ways, understanding that that very role is essential to effective school leadership can be your key to success. You have to become comfortable playing two roles simultaneously. You may be at the top of the decision-making pyramid in your school, but you're at the bottom of the decision-making pyramid as far as the school board, legislature, and superintendent's office is concerned. So, how do you effectively *lead from the middle*?

You do so, first of all, by understanding your core principles and nonnegotiables. What would you "go to the wall" for? What are the areas in which you can provide some flexibility to others?

Second, remember the advice often given by the athlete and activist Arthur Ashe (1943–1993): "Start where you are. Use what you have. Do what you can." Politics has sometimes been defined as *the art of the possible*. Since school leadership requires sharp political skills, it may be defined in the same way. It may not be possible to succeed every time that you and the superintendent disagree on a matter of policy, but if you start where you are, use what you have, and do what you can, your school will be much better off in the years to come.

Finally, if you haven't yet had a sincere discussion with your superintendent about his or her vision and priorities, do so at your earliest opportunity. Find out what motivates your supervisor the most. Get his or her perspective on your school's history and prospects. And then review your own vision for your school. Ask how that vision might help the superintendent advance what he or she hopes to achieve for the system.

Advisory Boards

Schools establish advisory boards for a large number of reasons. They may want insight into what local businesses or representatives of higher education want most from today's students. They may hope that the members of advisory boards will become donors to initiatives, booster clubs, and special projects. They may want to increase the visibility of the school in the community. In most cases, they hope to accomplish all three goals simultaneously.

But there is a principle about advisory boards that every school leader learns eventually: any time you put the word *advisory* in a group's title, that group will feel entitled to offer you advice, first on the issues within its charge, but eventually on any issue that it likes. Over time, advisory bodies often become more insistent that their advice be taken ("Why do you ask us for recommendations when you so rarely follow them?") and more willing to advise school leaders on matters that administrators and teachers may consider within their own purview ("Why aren't you getting rid of this teacher? We have a better candidate for you to consider.")

For this reason, many schools have stopped even using the term *advisory board*. Because many members of this group may have corporate backgrounds where the word *board* conveys a sense of decision-making authority, many schools are now calling these groups *advisory councils, bodies, circles, roundtables,* or *committees*. Similarly, board members are increasingly not referred to as *directors* but given such titles as *advisors, friends, supporters,* or *associates*.

When establishing a new advisory board, it's important to outline very clearly what the group is being asked to do (i.e., offer recommendations rather than make final decisions or implement policies) in which areas (i.e., athletics rather than curricular or personnel matters). Those expectations should be reinforced annually at an orientation meeting. It is easier to prevent misunderstandings than to address them once they arise.

If you encounter a small group of board members who regularly attempt to exceed their authority, meet with each person one on one to reexamine the board's specific responsibilities and where those responsibilities end. If the person cannot respect those boundaries, consider making a diplomatic suggestion that perhaps the person's talents are best applied to some area other than continued advisory board membership.

If the board itself has a priority that, although not in opposition to the mission and values the school has adopted, is clearly not of importance to you and other stakeholders, consider asking the board to fund that initiative itself. Sometimes merely stating that expectation will cause the advisory group to realize that it is making a recommendation that is not congruent with the school's current direction. At other times, they will come through with funding their priority for you.

Even though you may have preferred a contribution in another area, the project has the potential of being of at least some benefit, and you'll have made the members happy, perhaps even happy enough to continue funding initiatives of greater significance to your school.

The Business World

The local business community might put a different sort of pressure on schools from that of the other groups mentioned above. While school boards, superintendents, and legislatures are interested in pass rates and standardized test scores, businesses are primarily interested in potential employees who have the skills they need.

And those skills are often less academic than interpersonal in nature. Businesses frequently want schools to prepare students to show up for work on time, be committed to their jobs, have a positive attitude, communicate clearly both orally and in writing, think creatively, work well with others, manage their time effectively, be flexible and self-motivated, and avoid conflicts with their coworkers.

The challenge school leaders face is that there are only so many hours in a day but external constituents have almost unlimited expectations about what schools can do. The question "Why aren't our schools teaching students more about . . . ?" seems to be completed differently every day. For everyone who wants students to be better at handling their personal finances, there is someone else who wants them to be more knowledgeable about nutrition, local government, social media safety, mindfulness, first aid, self-defense, and myriad other skills and issues.

Businesses often see the world primarily in terms of their current needs or, more accurately, their *past* needs. The modern workplace is changing, just as schools are changing, and not all of today's students will have careers with set hours, mandated dress codes, or even a designated workplace itself. Increasing numbers of students will leave our schools to work in what is known as the "gig economy," an environment characterized by short-term contracts rather than long-term commitments to individual employers and freelance work rather than permanent jobs.

In order to remain relevant to these changing needs, schools have to prepare students for *both* traditional and nontraditional work environments. Privileging what some employers term "the soft skills" of dependability, decisiveness, and respect for authority may certainly benefit some students, but it could just as easily hold others back who will develop new ideas and create industries not yet imagined by challenging traditional ideas, being dissatisfied with the status quo, and creating a way of life in which their jobs no longer define who they are.

School leaders thus always remain teachers, even if they no longer have courses and students assigned to them. They teach corporate leaders, gently and with a great deal of diplomacy, about the many missions contemporary schools are trying to pursue. They describe their school's mission, vision, and values with complete understanding that the mission, vision, and values of local businesses will not be completely identical. They find areas or commonality where they can and articulately defend their differences where they must.

When businesses and corporate leaders want a specialized program, they can be asked, just like members of an advisory board are, to provide the funding for these initiatives since existing resources are already stretched thin. If the argument is made that existing funding should be reallocated, refer to the expectations that your other stakeholders—including those that provide that funding—have, not merely for the maintenance of those programs, but for their expansion.

Remember that the more suggestions business leaders give, the more resources you can request from them. A true partnership has to go both ways and can't exist simply by having one side create expectations while the other side fulfills them without additional support.

Representatives of Colleges and Universities

Like local businesses, representatives of colleges and universities often view your school only through the lens of what you can do for them. As school leaders, we can understand this tendency.

Elementary school teachers often say that preschool teachers should better prepare their students before they reach kindergarten or the first grade. Middle school teachers often say that elementary teachers should better prepare their students before they reach the sixth or seventh grade, and high school teachers often say that middle teachers should better prepare their students before they reach the ninth grade. So, it's no wonder that college and university professors often say that high school teachers should better prepare their students before they enter postsecondary education.

As with other external stakeholders, school leaders can address this pressure in part by educating representatives of colleges and universities about how well they are doing. Many postsecondary institutions are selective in the students they admit. Except for certain private schools, most institutions serving pre-K–12 students have a far broader range of students, many of whom come from families who are facing severe financial hardships, are sometimes indifferent or even hostile to the need for formal education, and have mental, physical, or emotional challenges that impede their progress.

Representatives of colleges and universities sometimes forget that preparing students for postsecondary education, while an important mission, is not a school's *sole* mission. Gently reminding them of this fact can be necessary.

The pressure that colleges and universities place on high schools often diminishes when a robust dual-enrollment program (an opportunity for currently enrolled high school students to take college courses, sometimes also known as a Move On When Ready program) is in place.

Colleges then receive a direct advantage from their active cooperation with schools: they receive additional student credit hours and often the tuition dollars that accompany them. One place to begin building a better alliance with postsecondary institutions is to create or expand a dual-enrollment program. Doing so places schools, colleges, and universities all "on the same side" and gives them a common goal of meeting students at their current levels of achievement and helping them progress further toward their goals.

Special Interest Groups

Every community (including the pre-K–12 educational community as a whole) contains special interest groups that want to advance a cause important to them. These groups may include those that are committed to gender or ethnic diversity, first or second amendment rights, particular religious or political views, and similar concerns.

School leaders often hear from special interest groups when they feel that their concerns haven't been addressed in matters of hiring or curricular development. Common questions from these groups may involve why there aren't more LGBTQ faculty members on the staff, why the history curriculum doesn't devote more attention to the displacement of Native American populations, why more books of the Bible aren't studied in literature and social studies courses, why scientific creationism or intelligent design isn't taught in earth sciences courses, and the like.

Special interest groups deserve to be taken seriously. Their causes are just as important to them as child development is to teachers and administrators. But taking a concern seriously does not mean that school leaders always have to accede to these groups' demands. The best response is almost always clear and open communication.

For example, the staffing of your school may already be more diverse than the group realizes, or filling a job opening may involve a delicate balance of matching qualifications, experience, and a broader array of diversity concerns than the group represents. At the moment, while diversity in sexual orientation may be important in your searches, ethnic diversity may need to take precedence because of the composition of your student body and the surrounding community.

At other times, because curricular goals are set by the state or school district, it may simply be impossible to set aside additional time for the issue of concern to the group. At private schools, that type of argument may not be possible, but you may be able to make your case in terms of your school's established mission, vision, and values.

Regardless of whether you work at a public or private institution, however, being dismissive of special interest groups is unlikely to be an effective strategy. Whether you support the group's cause or are philosophically opposed to it, the group's members are also members of your community. School leaders don't have to agree with all members of the community, but they do need to recognize the right of others to advocate for their vision with passion and sincerity.

Parents

Since interacting effectively with parents has been addressed in great detail in chapter 8 and will also be considered in chapter 10, it will be sufficient to say in the context of the current discussion that, although parents can be among a school leader's strongest allies, there are also times at which parents are also one of the groups that seeks to apply external pressure on administrators. A common tactic parents will use is to claim that they speak on behalf of many others when in fact they are only voicing their own opinions or those of one or two other people.

In the book *Shifting the Monkey* (2014), Todd Whitaker, a professor of educational leadership at the University of Missouri, describes a skillful way of interacting with those who claim to represent a large group. Tell the person that you want to be sensitive to the concerns of each person whom the parent claims to represent and ask for a list of their names so that you can call them individually.

In many cases, a list will never be forthcoming because the "large group" simply doesn't exist. In other cases, you'll probably end up with fewer than five people to call, most of whom aren't nearly as adamant about the issue as the representative claims (Whitaker 2014, 49–50).

Parents are almost always well intentioned, but they sometimes misinterpret situations because they've only heard about them from their children's perspectives, and those perspectives may not be accurate. Sometimes, too, parents may be one of those groups who remember their own school days more fondly than those days actually warrant. They can be skeptical of new ideas because they interpret these ideas in terms of their own experience, which may or may not be reflective of where your school is positioned right now.

It's beneficial, therefore, to bring as many parents to your school as possible so that you are exposed to a complete range of views. Idiosyncratic voices are, unfortunately, occasionally the loudest, and these voices become louder still when the only group a school leader hears from is not representative of the community as a whole. If it's difficult to get parents on campus to visit classes, at least bring them in for athletic or arts events. Use halftime and intermission to meet with them, hear their concerns, and express your vision.

ADVANCING YOUR OWN VISION

So far, the majority of this chapter has been devoted to some of the major external groups that tend to apply pressure on school leaders and recommendations about how to respond to that pressure. But ultimately, a school leader's goal should not be merely reacting to the vision of others. It should be advancing his or her own vision. How do you do that when it may seem at times as though everyone around you is trying to tell you what you should do next and how you should be doing your job?

Advancing your vision is easiest when it's not simply *your* vision but the vision of your school as a whole. That's why so much attention in these chapters has been devoted to articulating and building support for a shared mission, vision, and set of values. The more unified your school can be in promoting a clear identity and path forward, the more leverage you'll have in resisting unwanted pressure from outside the school.

The Education Trust has identified five key steps in the school improvement process.

1. *Diagnose.* Conduct a needs assessment to identify where growth needs to occur. The authors of this book would add to this recommendation from the Education Trust the advice presented in chapter 1: don't overlook appreciative inquiry in your desire to find areas of underperformance. The faculty and staff need to be reminded what they're doing well even as you hope your school will become even better in the future.
2. *Plan.* Identify specific strategies for improving student performance, school safety, and other key issues. Set target metrics where they are useful but remember that simply setting metrics is not the same thing

as developing a strategy. Planning means knowing *how* you'll proceed, not just *where* you're hoping to end up.

3. *Implement.* Put the plan into effect. Many school improvement processes go awry because the initial enthusiasm for them fades as other priorities emerge and day-to-day problems must be addressed. Remember that school improvement is a marathon, not a sprint. Long-term commitment is essential.

4. *Monitor.* Periodically confirm and report on your progress. Keep in mind that metrics, while useful as quantitative measures, are not the only source of information that exists. Make full use of qualitative measures such as reports by alumni, employers, other schools and colleges, community members, and parents about how your school has improved people's lives.

5. *Intensify action.* "Close the loop" on your improvement plan. If a strategy is working, expand it. If a strategy hasn't been as effective as you'd hoped, replace it. School improvement is a process, not a destination. You'll never get to a point where you'll be able to say "We did it, so now let's just maintain what we have right now." (The Education Trust n.d.)

School improvement processes work best when they're not imposed from above. Instead, the process should be top-down and bottom-up simultaneously. Initiate the process and maintain the enthusiasm from the administrative level, but generate ideas and empower implementation at the faculty and staff level. Be clear and candid if suggestions really don't align with your values and objectives, but always take those suggestions seriously.

Ask administrators, faculty members, and those on the staff the following guiding questions:

1. What's great about our school?
2. What's different about our school? In other words, how are we distinctive from other schools that people usually compare to us?
3. What do we want our school to look like ten years from now? Five years from now? Next year?
4. What should we be doing *now* to make our school look more like how we want it to look in the future?

FINAL OBSERVATIONS

Hearing suggestions from external stakeholders about how school leaders can do their jobs better and improve their schools is simply an inevitable aspect of school leadership. The higher you go in the educational hierarchy, the more you'll attract insights, recommendations, and complaints from people who believe they know what your priorities will be even better than you do.

The bad news is that external pressures can be extremely frustrating. They can leave you with days in which you feel as though no one approves of the way you're doing your job and that you're failing more often than you're succeeding. The good news is that sometimes your external constituents do actually make useful suggestions that you can capitalize on as part of your leadership strategy. But even when these suggestions are not particularly useful, listening to them attentively garners good will and may even lead to opportunities for external funding of initiatives.

What external pressures on schools and school leaders indicate is that what teachers and administrators do matters to people in their communities. Schools are never isolated enterprises. They're integral to the community in the way that certain clubs and even business entities may not be.

When people place pressure on you to make certain types of decisions, you have two choices. You can view it as unwanted interference and become frustrated, or you can view it as a reminder of how important school leadership is and take it as a compliment. If you choose the second course, you're more likely to find your work satisfying and to build stronger community relationships.

A CASE STUDY IN EXTERNAL PRESSURES ON SCHOOLS AND SCHOOL LEADERS

Barbara Seville is the former drama coach at your school. When her play, *The Marriage of Cyrano*, was optioned for a blockbuster film, Barbara could afford to resign from her teaching position and become a socialite in your community. She sometimes even refers to her new life as the local grande dame as "the role I was born to play."

Barbara's newly acquired wealth and social status have enabled her to win election to the school board. Since she was one of your former employees and helped build your school's drama program, she feels that she understands better than anyone how that program operates and how it should develop in the future.

Recently, the teacher you hired as Barbara's replacement has left your school (you suspect, although you're not sure, that his departure was largely due to Barbara's attempt to meddle in everything he did), and the position of drama coach is now vacant. As a member of the school board, Barbara has asked to serve on the search committee that will hire the new coach.

That development has you concerned, but your concern almost reaches the level of panic when, in a meeting with Barbara, you learn that she already has in mind the candidate she believes you should hire.

Her preferred candidate is one of her former students who, as you've learned from the principals of several other schools where he's worked, has a personality that can only be described as difficult. In other positions, he's already had numerous conflicts with parents, has proven to be inflexible as well as demanding, and (according to the performances you yourself have witnessed) doesn't seem to be a particularly good director.

You suspect that Barbara prefers this candidate largely because she believes, rightly or wrongly, that she can control him and thus influence the direction of your drama program.

What do you do?

DISCUSSION OF THE CASE STUDY

The situation outlined in this case study places you in a difficult position, since Barbara Seville is a member of the school board and, as was discussed in this chapter, the school board is in many ways your boss.

Your first attempt to improve the situation might be to flatter Barbara and say that, while you appreciate her willingness to serve, work on a hiring committee is quite time consuming and probably not the best use of her considerable talent. That strategy may not get you very far, but it is preferable to more open opposition due to Barbara's role and the inadvisability of causing her to become one of your professional opponents.

Your best resource in this case is probably the superintendent. He or she may be able to redirect Barbara's desire to be of service in ways that you can't. The superintendent may even be able to suggest that her best course of action is not to serve on the search committee, since that might appear to be a conflict of interest in light of her former work in the drama program, but to provide external funding for one or more of your school's productions. Giving Barbara a chance to be listed in the program as the producer or underwriter of a play may appeal to her more than merely choosing the next drama coach.

It is also possible that this is a situation in which special interest groups, rather than being a source of external pressure, can actually be one of your allies. If your faculty is not yet as diverse as you'd like in terms of gender, ethnicity, or some other factor, a community action group could help you make the case that other candidates besides Barbara's favored applicant need to be given serious consideration. If other principals are willing to go on the record about the difficulties caused at their schools by this applicant, you may be able to use this information for added support for your desire "not to narrow the applicant pool prematurely."

KEY POINTS IN THIS CHAPTER

- The external groups and stakeholders who may apply pressure on schools and school leaders include members of the school board, legislatures, the superintendent, members of advisory boards, people from the business world, representatives of colleges and universities, special interest groups, and parents.
- Those applying pressure are usually well intentioned, although they may not understand the full context of the situation in which your school is operating or all the goals you're trying to achieve.
- Some of these external stakeholders (notably the school board, legislature, and superintendent) are technically your boss, and so you must be very diplomatic in resisting any pressure they place on you to do things you don't regard as in your school's best interests.
- Often, external groups and stakeholders really just want to be heard. They don't always expect you to act on their advice, at least not immediately.
- External groups and stakeholders are sometimes responding to pressure they themselves have received from others. Therefore, they may see their obligations as having been fulfilled merely by raising the issue.
- Any group with the word *advisory* in its title may feel they have a license to advise you even about issues that aren't technically in its charter.
- While it can be frustrating to receive frequent recommendations and suggestions from external groups, school leaders can often use these situations as opportunities to increase good will or funding.
- The school improvement process and a persistent focus on the mission, vision, and values of the school are a school leader's best resources in resisting unwanted external pressure.

REFERENCES

The Education Trust. n.d. "The School Improvement Process." https://edtrust.org/students-cant-wait/school-improvement-process/

Levey, J. C., & Acker-Hocevar, M. 1998. *Site-Based Management: Retrospective Understandings and Future Directions*. Washington, DC: ERIC Clearinghouse.

Whitaker, T. 2014. *Shifting the Monkey: The Art of Protecting Good People from Liars, Criers, and Other Slackers*. Bloomington, IN: Solution Tree.

RESOURCES

Badowski, R., & Gittines, R. 2004. *Managing Up: How to Forge an Effective Relationship with Those above You.* New York, NY: Currency.

Baldoni, J. 2010. *Lead Your Boss: The Subtle Art of Managing Up.* New York, NY: AMA-COM.

Buller, J. L., & Reeves, D. M. 2018. *The Five Cultures of Academic Development: Crossing Boundaries in Higher Education Fundraising.* Washington, DC: CASE.

Conway, J., & Calz, F. 1995/1996. "The Dark Side of Shared Decision Making." *Educational Leadership* 53, 45–49.

David, J. 1995/1996. "The Who, What, and Why of Site-Based Management." *Educational Leadership* 53, 4–9.

Dobson, M. S., & Dobson, D. S. 2000. *Managing Up! 59 Ways to Build a Career-Advancing Relationship with Your Boss.* New York, NY: AMACOM.

Dufour, G. 2011. *Managing Your Manager: How to Get ahead with Any Type of Boss.* New York, NY: McGraw-Hill.

Matuson, R. C. 2011. *Suddenly in Charge: Managing Up, Managing Down, Succeeding All Around.* Boston, MA: Nicholas Brealey.

Odden, E., & Wohlstetter, P. 1995. "Making School-Based Management Work." *Educational Leadership* 52, 32–36.

Scott, G. G. 2006. *A Survival Guide for Working with Bad Bosses: Dealing with Bullies, Idiots, Back-Stabbers, and Other Managers from Hell.* New York, NY: AMACOM.

Smullen, F. W. 2014. *Ways and Means for Managing Up: 50 Strategies for Helping You and Your Boss Succeed.* New York, NY: McGraw-Hill.

Taylor, L. 2009. *Tame Your Terrible Office Tyrant (TOT): How to Manage Childish Boss Behavior and Thrive in Your Job.* Hoboken, NJ: Wiley.

Tulgan, B. 2010. *It's Okay to Manage Your Boss: The Step-by-Step Program for Making the Best of Your Most Important Relationship at Work.* San Francisco, CA: Jossey-Bass.

Useem, M. 2001. *Leading Up: How to Lead Your Boss so You Both Win.* New York, NY: Three Rivers Press.

Chapter Ten

Creating the Schools Today's Students Deserve

Ever since schools were first invented, administrators have been looking for a "magic potion," an utterly innovative approach that would make it possible for each student to reach his or her full potential, for administrators to employ only the best and brightest teachers who would be fully committed to the school's mission, and for the environment in which students learn and teachers instruct to be perfectly suited to their needs. It's unlikely that a single such "magic potion" will ever be found, but that doesn't mean that the question "What type of schools do today's students deserve?" can't be answered or isn't worth pursuing.

In his extended dialogue *The Republic*, the Greek philosopher Plato (ca. 427–347 BCE) explored a similar issue with regard to developing the type of government that people deserve. Plato's solution was to suggest that people first have to imagine the ideal or best possible form of government and then determine how actual states can be improved so that they will best approximate that goal. His leading questions thus became, "If you could design a system of government from the ground up, what would it be like? How would you create the perfect state so that it was ideally devoted to justice?"

For centuries now, philosophers have been critiquing Plato's answers to these questions, and those issues extend far beyond the scope of this book, but his method remains intriguing for leaders who are interested in creating the types of schools that today's students need and deserve. If you could design a school from the ground up, what would it be like? How would you create the perfect learning environment so that it was ideally devoted to student success?

Although as Plato learned all too well through his own efforts to put his theories into practice in the Sicilian town of Syracuse, perfection is never really attainable. But if you start by imagining the features that would be found in the *best imaginable* school, you then may be able to adapt some of them into the *best possible* school, thus creating improvements that would never have been conceivable if you hadn't dared to dream beyond what is currently accepted as the *best available*.

In addition, you can learn from those rare experiences where what might be dismissed as impossible actually proved feasible after all. In fewer than eight months, one of this book's coauthors was able to create a school from little more than a great idea, an educational philosophy that focused on best practices and innovative new ideas, a leadership team that was motivated to achieve something that had never been done before, and a commitment to creating the best possible learning environment for all the students the school would serve.

The formula for that school's success should come as no surprise to anyone who has read the previous chapters. It began with a focus on mission and culture, was developed by using the right approaches to hiring precisely the right faculty and staff, adopted a consensus-based approach to the creation of a curriculum that was balanced and dynamic, and devoted itself to continual success by emphasizing the best in all its members, not simply a series of problems that needed to be solved.

Most readers of this book will never have a similar opportunity to design their own schools, but by reflecting on the question, "If I could design the best possible school, what would it be like?" you can begin to identify the components that are most likely to lead to schools that today's students deserve. So, what might those components include?

SCHOOL LEADERS

In order to be as effective as possible, school leaders have to embody the mission, culture, and values that they claim are essential for student success. In order to achieve this goal, school leaders have to strive to be as supportive, compassionate, consistent, open-minded, confident about the future, and flexible as possible. They need to set clear expectations for themselves, their students, and those who work at the school and then demonstrate in everything they say and do their conviction that people can live up to those expectations. They must demonstrate integrity, transparency, and a willingness to listen to other perspectives.

If it's your goal to be this kind of school leader, you can start by looking at your school's current mission statement. Is it accurate, distinctive, and ambitious? If not, revisit the mission statement by reviewing the practice of appreciative inquiry as outlined in the first chapter of this book. If the statement is indeed accurate, distinctive, and ambitious, are you living up to those principles every day? Do your teachers, parents, and students know and understand your mission?

Developing the mission, culture, and values of a school is a never-ending process. It starts at faculty meetings when school leaders ask teachers to describe the school's mission in their own words. If you engage in this practice, don't correct or reject any answer immediately. Even responses that are dramatically different from what you believe the school's mission should be are informative; they tell you where people's minds are now so that you'll better understand where they need to go.

Once you've developed with the faculty and staff a consensus-based statement of mission and culture, do something similar for your shared vision ("Where do we want to go? What do we want to change?") and values ("What are our core principles? What do we never want to change?"). Then publish these statements in ways that everyone can see.

It's not important that people can recite the statements word for word. It's more important that people understand them, talk about them, and embody them in their practices. Remember the point raised in the first chapter of this book: effective school leaders create a culture in which school-improvement initiatives are teacher-led. School leaders do not make good schools great on their own.

Many leaders find it valuable to engage periodically in "mission moments" as school-wide activities. A mission moment occurs when all the students in the school engage in an activity that fosters the school's mission or reflect its values.

Suppose a school has a mission that states, "Creative thinking is one of our most important values, and we seek to think creatively in all our activities." One week's mission moment might be for each class to conduct a small project that requires creative thinking.

One class might strategize about new ways to promote recycling. Another might explore how the methods used in one discipline (such as hypothesis testing) might be adapted to a different discipline (such as music appreciation or the study of literature). A third class might develop a list titled "Ten Things I Can Do Each Day to Alleviate Homelessness." Photos and videos of these mission moments would then promote continued enthusiasm for the school's values, document the success of the activity, and give both students and teachers a sense of pride in what they have done.

Developing the type of culture that is needed in today's schools doesn't happen overnight. It rarely even happens in a single year. Because members of the faculty and staff rarely accept new ideas until they trust administrators and understand their commitment to everyone's best interests, noticeable improvements in mission, culture, and values may seem unbearably slow at first, but once school leaders demonstrate that they have integrity, the members of the school community who must implement essential changes will begin to come on board.

There may be a few initial supporters at first, then a few more members of the faculty and staff will come around, then a few more, and then finally a tipping point will be reached, and the change that once appeared slow will now seem to be very rapid. Leaders have to view this process as a long-term investment in the needs of their students and not as a short-term way of advancing their careers.

PARENTS

The mind-set of parents also evolves quite slowly. Many parents think of school only in terms of their own experience and the needs of their own children. In order for parents to see the larger picture of what the school is trying to accomplish, communication with them must be transparent, constant, and two-way. An added advantage of the mission moments described earlier is that these activities can be shared with parents via newsletters, blogs, meetings, email blasts, and other means that demonstrate the successes that are happening at the school every day.

Parents love to see pictures of their children. Photographs and videos of what students are accomplishing can be a very effective way of educating parents about the progress your school is making. They, in turn, will help carry this message to others. Once parents come to embrace the mission and vision of the school, they will amplify this message and be your most valuable agents in communicating the school's values to the broader community.

At the same time, parents can be a wonderful source of insights and information. Listen to their concerns. Be understanding of their hopes and dreams for their children. Sometimes parents just want to know that their voices are being heard. At other times they may misunderstand what you are trying to accomplish, and a candid dialogue can clear up these misconceptions. At other times they bring valuable new perspectives that are important for you to see.

An observation that is often attributed, correctly or not, to the retired rear admiral Marsha Johnson ("Marty") Evans states that "if you think you know it all, you are not listening." People stop paying attention when they think they already know the answers. A school leader can't afford to fall into this trap. He or she must be willing to listen to others to gain as much knowledge as possible to help guide the school forward. One of the most important sources of insight you'll have as a school leader is the parents of your students.

Parental willingness to be involved in school activities sometimes varies by type of institution. Parents are often more willing to become involved in private schools than public schools, and the willingness they had to become engaged when their children were in elementary or middle school may wane by the time their children are in high school.

As a result, school leaders have to make it a priority to promote parental involvement at those institutions where it's lacking. Through the guidance department, schools can sponsor themed nights focusing on specific educational goals, career planning, and common student challenges.

If parents won't come to school leaders, the school leaders may have to go to them. They may need to reach out and partner with parents in finding strategies for more thoroughly engaging the entire family in the educational process and in creating opportunities for parents to familiarize themselves with the curriculum. A combined effort involving social media, the school website, and traditional mailings and newsletters is often the best way to highlight the achievements that are occurring at the school and communicate any needed information.

In sum, communication with parents must be an open exchange of views. You won't always see eye to eye with them, but you also won't know if they have any legitimate concerns if you aren't receptive to their ideas.

STUDENTS

Like parents, students deserve frequent two-way conversation. Too many school leaders believe that a school's mission is something *told* to students, not co-created with them. But administrators who are interested in the long-term development of the school talk to their students. They ask them why they like the school and what makes them proud to be students there.

In many cases, what the students say has close parallels to the mission and values that the school leaders hope to promote. But when that doesn't happen, leaders have an excellent opportunity to understand how their own conception of what the school is and can be isn't shared by their most important stakeholder group.

That experience can be humbling, but it can also be highly revealing: It gives school leaders a chance to evaluate whether their vision of the future is really meeting the needs of those who will be embodying that future. Perhaps the leaders' goals weren't articulated in ways that resonated with those whom the school serves. Perhaps those goals didn't reflect what the students need but only what others *assumed* the students need. Perhaps both the leaders and the students are interested in the same things but using different vocabulary to describe their goals.

Whatever the case may be, administrators will never determine how best to proceed if they always talk but never listen to students. What students say they want shouldn't always be granted, but it should at least be heard.

MEMBERS OF THE COMMUNITY

With social media pervading all aspects of life today, schools are fortunate to have an opportunity to communicate openly and regularly with members of the community. In many ways, social media is a form of "free advertising" for schools: it helps them get their message out when they want, in the way they want, and with the efficiency they want.

Even if members of the community never send their children to the school, they are an important audience for school leaders. Community members vote on tax levies, elect representatives who decide on important issues, and serve on school boards. So, it can be valuable for leaders to convey a consistent and exciting message of what the school's mission is.

In conveying a message to the public, it's important to remember that everyone today is inundated with information and attempts by others to "sell" them something. People don't have time to read long white papers that address the school's vision for the future or to attend PowerPoint presentations on educational policy. Members of the community need concise messages that capture their attention and are easy to remember.

On social media sites, use appropriate hashtags such as the name of the school or an important aspect of your mission like #criticalthinking or #preparingfutureleaders so that your message will be easier to find and share. (For recommendations on how to craft messages that are effective and easily remembered, see Heath and Heath, 2007.)

NOT EVERYONE WILL BE ON BOARD

Once the school's mission has been developed, widespread support has been achieved, and a consistent message has been conveyed to various stakeholder groups, the next question many school leaders ask is, "How do I get the people on board who are still resisting this vision or even attempting to undermine it?"

The simple (but perhaps counterintuitive) answer is you don't. One of the mistakes that school leaders make is thinking that absolutely every member of the faculty and staff needs to be fully supportive of a new vision before starting to make that vision a reality. As a result, they become bogged down in trying to persuade a few critical people instead of moving forward and demonstrating the power of the new vision.

In any change initiative, members of an organization generally fall into three groups. The *early adopters* are those who are immediately excited about new ideas and want to participate in pilot programs to test them out. *Fellow travelers* don't support the new initiatives as quickly as early adopters but eventually become supporters when they see that the change will be less difficult or the benefits more significant than they originally thought. *Resisters* oppose change of any kind because it takes them outside their comfort zone and threatens their self-image as highly competent, successful professionals.

The process of moving a change initiative forward is to embrace the early adopters as equals, continue to win over the fellow travelers by repeated discussions of mission and goals, and not to be distracted by the resisters. The early adopters are a school leader's best advocates in promoting support for a vision. They talk eagerly about all the wonderful things that are happening in their classes, and some of their enthusiasm begins to attract the fellow travelers.

As the core group of committed supporters begins to grow, one of two things will happen to the resisters. Some of them will accept the new vision as inevitable; their acceptance may be grudging and hesitant at first, but it will grow as the new vision proves its value. Others of the resisters will never be won over, and it's a waste of effort to try persuading them. They will find themselves gradually more isolated in their resistance and, within two or three years, will retire, accept positions elsewhere, or simply give up their vocal opposition.

It can take patience as this process plays out until the school reaches that tipping point mentioned earlier, after which the changes that had once seemed slow in coming will begin to occur more and more rapidly. Before that tipping point occurs, it's useful to remember the point raised by Carol Dweck, the Lewis and Virginia Eaton Professor of Psychology at Stanford University, in her book *Mindset: The New Psychology of Success* (2008).

Dweck notes that people tend to have one of two primary mind-sets: a *fixed mind-set* that views intelligence and other abilities as commodities ("You either have them or you don't,") or a *growth mind-set* that views intelligence and other abilities as capabilities ("You can develop them further through exercise and practice"). Teachers with a growth mind-set will be actively trying to understand how the school's mission and vision will help students. Those with a fixed mind-set will just assume that they can wait you out. If they can stall long enough, they believe, the proposed changes will simply go away.

The best time to discuss mission with members of the faculty and staff is in conjunction with their annual evaluations or in meetings where annual goals are set. In such a setting, you can outline your expectations and ask people whether they feel that they can meet them. Doing so deprives naysayers of the opportunity to claim that you never made it clear what you expected them to do before they signed their contracts. These conversations should never be confrontational; they should be conducted with respect and out of a desire to be helpful. For this reason, the question, "How can I support you?" should always be part of these sessions.

Demonstrating support goes a long way with teachers. Follow up your meeting with a memo of understanding about what you discussed and agreed to. If necessary or desirable, consider scheduling monthly check-in meetings where these conversations can continue. In many cases, once people see that you really do have their best interests at heart, even those who were initially resistant to the new mission become supporters.

If they don't, you can have a follow-up conversation during the next year's review session. Ask the person, "How did it feel this year living out the school's mission as we discussed in our last meeting?" or "Is the school's mission something you feel you can demonstrate each day? How would you do that?"

If, after a number of these discussions, the person is still so opposed to the principles that others have agreed to, it may be necessary to talk about whether the fit between the school and the employee is beneficial to both parties and, if not, what options exist. If you do decide to transfer or nonrenew the employee, that process needs to be done with respect and grace. Even those members of the faculty and staff who are no longer advancing the mission of the school have poured their heart and soul into trying to help the students. Regardless of whether you agree with the methods they used to achieve those ends, in their minds, they did the best they could.

SHOWING GENUINE APPRECIATION

Some schools have only a few members of the faculty and staff, while others employ hundreds. Nevertheless, to whatever extent possible, school leaders should set themselves the goal of interacting at least once a day with every teacher, even if it is only to say hello. By greeting every teacher every day, school leaders demonstrate genuine appreciation for what the teachers do and make an often-difficult job feel more rewarding.

Whenever they can, effective leaders also sit in on different classes for several minutes, not to evaluate the teacher but to demonstrate their support for the learning process. After the visit, an email or a personal note can reinforce this message of appreciation. For example, imagine the impact of a handwritten message like the following on a teacher who is doing her best for her students.

Dear Ms. Mentor,

It was such a pleasure visiting your classroom today. I was very impressed by what I saw in the excerpts your students performed from *Julius Caesar*. Watching the confidence with which they spoke publicly truly supports our mission of preparing our students to be leaders of tomorrow. I hope to have another opportunity soon.

Such a message demonstrates true appreciation for the teacher's efforts. It isn't overly generic ("Thanks for all you do"), and it doesn't depend on the leader's personal feelings about the teacher. Rather, it is tied directly to the mission and culture of the school ("supports our mission of preparing our students to be leaders of tomorrow") and mentions a specific activity that the leader witnessed.

Interactions of this kind demonstrate how administrators can lead with vision and appreciation, not decrees or the mere enforcement of policies. The teachers feel validated in their efforts to carry out the mission of the school.

Additionally, when it's time for a formal annual evaluation, the teacher who has been observed knows that the leader has seen them multiple times throughout the year. He or she won't feel intimidated by an administrator's single visit to a class. And there won't be the false belief that success or failure depends on the administrator's whim or what happens to occur on the one day that was selected for a formal classroom observation.

If you're truly interested in transforming the culture of a school, this process can go even further. Just as every member of the faculty and staff should be greeted, so should every student. That goal may seem impossible in large institutions, but creative approaches can make even the impossible possible.

Design a rotation schedule for each week that allows you to greet different students at different entrances or at different grade levels. Engage the assistant principals and division heads in a collective effort to greet each student individually.

Teachers, too, should be encouraged to greet each student by name when that student arrives for the day. In environments where it is appropriate, the student can also be welcomed with a handshake or fist bump. Smiles are, of course, always appropriate, and saying goodbye to each student at the end of the day is also an effective way of building community spirit.

If you believe that you'll never have time for what may seem such a superficial activity, remember this: interacting with each person individually is a basic strategy for creating a positive school culture and fulfilling your school's mission, and there's nothing more important than that. School leaders have time for the activities that seem critical to them, and embodying the desired culture is the most critical job.

In addition, you'll have the time because these personal conversations will reduce the number of fires you need to put out. You'll have the time because everyone on your team will now be driving the school's mission. What you're doing is simply reallocating your workload from having to deal with managerial issues to having more opportunities to elevate your school. You will find the way in which you spend your day is different (and more productive) because everyone will come to understand and live the school's mission.

Other ways of advancing this mission is by using podcasts, YouTube, and similar services to record weekly teacher and student shout-outs. Distributing the links to these recordings throughout the school, as well as to parents and school board members, helps reinforce your message and builds school spirit. Instead of feeling frustrated because of the number of times that you have to reprimand someone for doing what they shouldn't be doing, you'll find yourself energized by praising people for doing exactly the sorts of things that they should be doing.

Some school leaders have shown genuine appreciation for the faculty and staff by instituting a practice known as the Friday huddle. After the students leave the school on Friday, all members of the faculty and staff meet together briefly. The principal recognizes a few individuals for good performance (making sure not to praise the same people too often so that others think they're being treated unfairly), make a few announcements, and then let everyone go home a few minutes early. The Friday huddle is a cost-free way of saying, "I recognize the excellent work that you do, and I appreciate it. I also recognize that you have lives outside of work, so I want you to have a little extra free time to enjoy them."

PROFESSIONAL LEARNING COMMUNITIES

The concept of the Professional Learning Community (PLC) has already proven its value as an approach for school improvement. As discussed by such authors as Richard and Rebecca Dufour, Robert Eaker, Sharon Kramer, Sarah Schuhl, Anthony Muhammad, and others, a PLC is a group of teachers who meet regularly to improve their pedagogical skills and enhance student learning (DuFour, DuFour, Eaker, Many, and Mattos 2016; Dufour 1997; Kramer and Schuhl 2017; Muhammad 2017).

Sometimes also known by other names—such as teaching circles, communities of practice, and collaborative learning groups—PLCs are a combination of mutual support groups, continuing education opportunities, experience sharing networks, and mechanisms for ongoing professional dialogue. Participants often feel that PLCs are more effective than many other in-service training programs because they encourage peers to support one another rather than rely on outside consultants who may not understand the unique challenges faced by teachers in that particular school.

A PLC tends to work best when its participants share a common experience, such as teaching the same grade level or working in the same academic discipline. Some PLCs also function a bit like book clubs, with a common text (usually involving an innovative pedagogical strategy or an issue involving a current opportunity or challenge in education) guiding the discussion of the members.

School leaders may find that PLCs serve as useful vehicles for reinforcing a consistent message about school mission and culture as well as a highly cost-effective means of providing ongoing training. Particularly during periods when a new vision is being developed at the school, well-designed PLCs can be where that vision is co-created as part of a collaborative process in which values are shared and mutually agreeable goals are explored (Dufour and Eaker 2008).

PLCs help school leaders avoid the pitfalls of becoming so obsessed with data that they make decisions merely in order to achieve artificial benchmarks rather than on the basis of what makes the best sense in their individual environments. They encourage the development of improvement plans that are teacher led, student oriented, and data informed. There is then less need to encourage buy-in because ideas for necessary change aren't imposed from above but rather emerge more naturally by consensus among the very stakeholders who will need to implement those changes.

Even though initiatives originate at the level of the PLC, it remains important for administrators and department heads to provide support, guidance, and monitoring in order to ensure that the teachers and students have what they'll need in order to meet the established goals. Regular checkpoints throughout the year should be set when teachers will share their progress with supervisors and assess their results. School leaders must always be aware of any action steps planned at the program level and be visible inside the classroom to reinforce the school's commitment to its vision.

In this way, school improvement becomes a part of each person's standard operating procedure. Goals are periodically reassessed by each department, the school-wide leadership team, and other constituencies as appropriate. Professional learning sessions for all school personnel should be tied to meeting the established school improvement goals through improvement of the curriculum (setting and implementing high standards), instruction (sharing effective classroom teaching strategies), and assessment (adopting both formative and summative review processes, as discussed in chapter 4).

By encouraging participation in PLCs, school leaders make it much easier for teachers to work collaboratively with them in the process of improving instruction in all classes.

FINAL OBSERVATIONS

The position of school leader offers you many opportunities each day to make decisions that affect dozens, perhaps hundreds of people. It is essential for anyone pursuing a leadership position in education to make decisions ethically, always focusing on what's best for the students.

Not only must school leaders work within the law, but they must also model honesty, transparency, vision, fairness, compassion, and equity in every decision they make. It's vital for school leaders to share their vision and values with students, parents, teachers, and all other stakeholders in the school community.

One of the most important qualities any academic leader can have is being reflective. A successful principal or head of school is someone who embraces learning as a lifelong process, and the chief administrator must be the lead learner in the school so that he or she can model how continuous improvement starts with the staff.

Nevertheless, none of this positive development is likely to occur if school leaders don't take to heart the central premise of this book: all good things start from the school leader's unwavering focus on culture, values, and mission.

A CASE STUDY IN CREATING MISSION-DRIVEN SCHOOLS

Hope S. Eternal was recently appointed to serve as the principal of Fallen Arches High School. Although Fallen Aches has much to be proud of, Hope finds that the school is sadly lacking in team spirit and a sense of collective purpose. Each academic division has developed a strong silo mentality. The turnover rate for teachers is unacceptably high. Students rarely demonstrate a sense of pride in attending the school. And attendance at concerts, plays, and athletic events rarely consists of anyone other than the students who happen to be involved in that activity.

When Hope speaks to members of the faculty and staff, they tell her that things have always been that way. People in the community relate similar impressions.

Fallen Arches was a consolidated school formed when three older high schools in the area were closed and the students were moved to the newly constructed Fallen Arches campus. The facilities of the former high schools were aging, and a decline in the school-age population made a single regional high school the only financially feasible option. But many of the students (and even their parents) had developed affection for their former schools and, in the words of the superintendent, "the whole idea of Fallen Arches never really took off." What could Hope do to begin remedying this situation?

DISCUSSION OF THE CASE STUDY

Consolidated schools often suffer from an identity crisis for the very reason suggested by this scenario. The students who attend them, perhaps reflecting the attitude of their parents, may have developed a sense of identity with their former school. The new school, in their minds, is not "their" school, and so the sense of communal spirit one frequently finds in school communities may be lacking.

Hope's predecessor(s) had an opportunity that they clearly wasted. They could have followed the guidelines outlined in this chapter about what school leaders can do when designing a school from the ground up. They could have worked collaboratively with the incoming teachers and students to select team names, mascots, titles for the school newspaper and yearbook, and other elements of the school's culture that would help make them feel they "own" the school.

They could have held discussions with stakeholders about what the best possible school for the future might be and then incorporated as many of those suggestions as would have been feasible. They could have begun with a focus on mission and culture, hired precisely the right faculty and staff to embody those values, adopted a consensus-based approach to the creation of an innovative curriculum, and continually emphasized the best in all its students, faculty, and staff.

Since those steps were not taken, however, Hope has to turn around a struggling culture rather than begin with a dynamic one. Her message could be something like this: "Because I'm new here and because it's been a few years since Fallen Arches High School developed its mission and vision, now seems like a good time for us as a community to revisit some important issues. What do we want to be for the future? What do we believe might be possible? How would we go about creating the sort of high school that we dream of?"

Developing new, consensus-based statements of mission, vision, and values from these conversations could be an important first step in Hope's renewal plan. Those statements could be posted at key points throughout the school. The students might even be encouraged to develop their own code of expectations that outlines not the things they can't do because they'd lead to sanctions but their hopes for what they can become as a community. This type of code of expectations might look like the following:

> We, the students of Fallen Arches High School, pledge to uphold the highest values of integrity at our school and in our community. We will respect one another as individuals, work for the common good, and strive always to do what is right. We will be honest and honorable both in our academic work and in our lives and deserve the trust that is given us. We will think critically, pursue the truth, develop our own creativity, and act to make our world a better place.

Hope might consider instituting a new convocation ceremony at the start of each year. All students would stand and recite their pledge together. Then new students would come forward and sign their names into a ledger, officially registering them as scholars of Fallen Arches High School.

Hope could end the ceremony by saying, "And now that you have committed to these high principles and registered your name among all the students of Fallen Arches High School, I am proud as your principal to welcome you officially to our community." The convocation would thus be what anthropologists call a liminal event or rite of passage, an activity that marks the start of a new identity in the community.

By sharing mission moments with parents and members of the larger community, Hope could reinforce the new vision that she creates at the school. In her written and oral remarks to faculty, staff, and students, she could reinforce the importance of the school's mission in the choices made by everyone in the Fallen Arches family.

Additionally, she could speak one-on-one with members of the faculty and staff to gauge each person's level of support for the mission. She could highlight the work of her "early adopters," praising them publicly, treating them as her equals, and letting others be inspired by their example. As she, her assistant principals, and division heads make it a point to greet each student individually as he or she arrives in the morning, the school will gradually come to feel like a special place, one in which everyone takes pride.

KEY POINTS IN THIS CHAPTER

- In order to create the *best possible* school, it is often useful to begin by reflecting on what the *best imaginable* school would be.
- School leaders should set clear expectations for themselves, their students, and those who work at the school and then demonstrate in everything they say and do their conviction that everyone can live up to those expectations.
- Statements of mission, culture, and values should be developed by consensus among a broad cross section of the school's stakeholders and then published in all school manuals and posted throughout the school.
- Mission moments are occasions when all the students in the school engage in an activity that fosters the school's mission or reflects its values. Photographs, videos, and descriptions of these mission moments should be shared widely because they help to build a sense of community.
- Discussions of mission and culture with faculty, staff, and students should truly be two-way conversations. They should not merely consist of the school leader trying to persuade others to support the mission.
- Not everyone who works at the school will be on board with the new mission (at least not initially), and that's OK. Change is difficult for many

people, and everyone should be treated with respect and support before deciding whether or not they're a good fit for the school's new mission.

• Showing genuine appreciation requires a personal touch, such as greeting each member of the faculty and staff (and, if possible, each student) individually on a daily basis.

REFERENCES

Dufour, R. 1997. "Schools as Learning Communities: Functioning as Learning Communities Enables Schools to Focus on Student Achievement." *Journal of Staff Development 18*(2): 56–57.

DuFour, R., & E. Eaker. 2008. *Professional Learning Communities at Work: New Insights for Improving Schools.* Bloomington, IN: National Educational Service.

DuFour, R., R. DuFour, R. Eaker, T. W. Many, & M. Mattos. 2016. *Learning by Doing: A Handbook for Professional Learning Communities at Work* (3rd ed.). Bloomington, IN: Solution Tree.

Dweck, C. S. 2008. *Mindset: The New Psychology of Success.* New York, NY: Ballantine Books.

Heath, C., & D. Heath. 2007. *Made to Stick: Why Some Ideas Survive and Others Die.* New York, NY: Random House.

Kramer, S. V., & S. Schuhl. 2017. *School Improvement for All: How-to Guide for Doing the Right Work.* Bloomington, IN: Solution Tree.

Muhammad, A. 2018. *Transforming School Culture: How to Overcome Staff Division.* Bloomington, IN: Solution Tree.

RESOURCES

Dance, S. D. 2018. *Deliberate Excellence: Three Fundamental Strategies That Drive Educational Leadership.* Thousand Oaks, CA: Corwin.

Kim, A., A. Gonzales-Black, & K. Lai. 2018. *The NEW School Rules: 6 Vital Practices for Thriving and Responsive Schools.* Thousand Oaks, CA: Corwin.

Klimek, K. J., E. Ritzenhein, & K. Sullivan. 2008. *Generative Leadership: Shaping New Futures for Today's Schools.* Thousand Oaks: Corwin Press.

Robinson, K., & L. Aronica. 2016. *Creative Schools: The Grassroots Revolution That's Transforming Education.* New York, NY: Penguin.

Ubben, G. C., L. W. Hughes, & C. J. Norris. 2017. *The Principal: Creative Leadership for Excellence in Schools* (8th ed.). Boston, MA: Pearson.

Other Books by Jeffrey L. Buller

- *A Handbook for College and University Advisory Boards* (with Dianne M. Reeves)
- *Mindful Leadership: An Insight-Based Approach to College Administration*
- *Authentic Academic Leadership: A Values-Based Approach to College Administration*
- *The Five Cultures of Academic Development: Crossing Boundaries in Higher Education Fundraising* (with Dianne M. Reeves)
- *Hire the Right Faculty Member Every Time: Best Practices in Recruiting, Selecting, and Onboarding College Professors*
- *Best Practices for Faculty Search Committees: How to Review Applications and Interview Candidates*
- *Going for the Gold: How to Become a World-Class Academic Fundraiser* (with Dianne M. Reeves)
- *World-Class Fundraising Isn't a Solo Sport: The Team Approach to Academic Fundraising* (with Dianne M. Reeves)
- *A Toolkit for College Professors* (with Robert E. Cipriano)
- *A Toolkit for Department Chairs* (with Robert E. Cipriano)
- *Building Leadership Capacity: A Guide to Best Practices* (with Walter H. Gmelch)
- *Change Leadership in Higher Education: A Practical Guide to Academic Transformation*
- *Positive Academic Leadership: How to Stop Putting Out Fires and Start Making a Difference*
- *Best Practices in Faculty Evaluation: A Practical Guide for Academic Leaders*

- *Academic Leadership Day By Day: Small Steps That Lead to Great Success*
- *The Essential Department Chair: A Comprehensive Desk Reference*, second edition
- *The Essential Academic Dean: A Comprehensive Desk Reference*, second edition
- *The Essential College Professor: A Practical Guide to an Academic Career*

More about ATLAS

ATLAS: Academic Training, Leadership, & Assessment Services offers training programs, books, and materials dealing with collegiality and positive academic leadership. Its more than fifty highly interactive programs include the following:

- Introduction to Academic Leadership
- Team Building for Academic Leaders
- Time Management for Academic Leaders
- Stress Management for Academic Leaders
- Budgeting for Academic Leaders
- Decision Making for Academic Leaders
- Problem Solving for Academic Leaders
- Conflict Management for Academic Leaders
- Emotional Intelligence for Academic Leaders
- Effective Communication for Academic Leaders
- Work-Life Balance for Academic Leaders
- Best Practices in Academic Fundraising
- Protecting Yourself from a Toxic Work Environment
- Developing Leadership Capacity: How You Can Create a Leadership Development Program at Your Institution
- We've Got to Stop Meeting Like This: Leading Meetings Effectively

- Why Academic Leaders Must Lead Differently: Understanding the Organizational Culture of Higher Education
- Getting Organized: Taking Control of Your Schedule, Workspace, and Habits to Get More Done in Less Time with Lower Stress
- Collegiality and Teambuilding
- Change Leadership in Higher Education
- Promoting Faculty and Staff Engagement
- Best Practices in Faculty Recruitment and Hiring
- Best Practices in Faculty Evaluation
- Best Practices in Coaching and Mentoring
- Moving Forward: Training and Development for Advisory Boards
- Training the Trainers: How to Give Presentations and Provide Training the ATLAS Way
- Managing Up for Academic Leaders: How to Flourish When Dealing with Your Boss and Your Boss's Boss
- Creating a Culture of Student Success
- Positive Academic Leadership: How to Stop Putting Out Fires and Start Making a Difference
- Authentic Academic Leadership: A Values-Based Approach to Academic Leadership
- Mindful Academic Leadership: A Mindfulness-Based Approach to Academic Leadership
- Fostering a College University: An In-Depth Exploration of Collegiality in Higher Education
- Managing Conflict: An In-Depth Exploration of Conflict Management in Higher Education
- A Toolkit for College Professors
- A Toolkit for Department Chairs
- Exploring Academic Leadership: Is College/University Administration Right for Me?

ATLAS offers programs in half-day, full-day, and multiday formats. ATLAS also offers reduced prices on leadership books and sells materials that can be used to assess your institution or program:

- the Collegiality Assessment Matrix (CAM), which allows academic programs to evaluate the collegiality and civility of their faculty members in a consistent, objective, and reliable manner
- the Self-Assessment Matrix (S-AM), which is a self-evaluation version of the CAM
- the ATLAS Campus Climate and Moral Survey
- the ATLAS Faculty and Staff Engagement Survey

These assessment instruments are available in both electronic and paper formats. In addition, the ATLAS eNewsletter addresses a variety of issues related to academic leadership and is sent free to subscribers.

For more information, contact:

ATLAS: Academic Training, Leadership, & Assessment Services
9154 Wooden Road
Raleigh, NC 27617
   800-355-6742
   www.atlasleadership.com
   Email: questions@atlasleadership.com

Index

active shooter scenarios, 19; administrator approach in, 24; gateway behaviors warning in, 25; in school safety, 20; sign-in system and name tag requirement in, 24; someone already known involvement in, 24; student safety in, 25; teacher training on warning signs in, 25

ADD. *See* attention-deficit disorder

ADHD. *See* attention-deficit/hyperactivity disorder

advisory boards: advice entitlement of, 135; clear expectations for, 135; initiative funding by, 136; reasons for establishing, 135; specific responsibilities reexamination in, 135–136; term use and, 135

Alcala, Leah, 103

Apfel, N., 54

appreciative inquiry, 5, 9–10, 12–13, 16, 148; best times identification in, 6; deploy in, 7; design in, 6; discover in, 6; distinctive assets in, 7; dream in, 6; engagement in, 7; list posting in, 7–8; observation removal in, 7; strengths and points of pride identification in, 7

Aristotle, 8, 9

Ashe, Arthur, 134

Association for Psychological Sciences, 65

attention-deficit disorder (ADD), 94

attention-deficit/hyperactivity disorder (ADHD), 94

Barbe, Walter Burke, 65

Baumrind, Diana, 121–122, 123

Borum, R., 20

"Boy Who Cried Wolf Syndrome", 23

Bracey, Gerald, 108, 110

Breaux, Annette, 90, 91

Brown, Rita Mae, 72–73

Brzustoski, P., 54

bullying: community-wide discussion about, 26–27; conflict resolution techniques in, 27; constructive behavior demonstration in, 27; first response in, 26; home issues in, 26; physical abuse in, 26; power use in, 26; punishment and, 26; social or relational abuse in, 26; verbal abuse in, 26; younger students discussions in, 27. *See also* cyberbullying

business community: corporate leader teaching in, 137; "gig economy" change in, 136–137; initiatives funding of, 137; interpersonal skills need of, 136; potential employees interest of, 136; traditional and nontraditional work environments in, 137; unlimited expectations of, 136

Tennessee Comprehensive Assessment
  Program, 99
TKES. *See* Teacher Keys Effectiveness
  System

US Public Law 107-110, 99

Van Brunt, B., 20
Veenman, Marcel, 64
video game versus school experience, 69;
  immersion in, 70; narrative in, 69–70;
  personal best in, 70; progress in, 69;
  social facilitation in, 70
vision, advancing own: close loop on, 141;
  guiding questions for, 141;
  implementation of, 141; needs
  assessment in, 140; progress reports in,

141; school community sharing in, 140;
  school improvement steps in, 140–141;
  school leader goal of, 140; student
  performance improvement strategies
  identification in, 140–141; top-down
  and bottom-up process in, 141
Vossekuil, B., 20

Weber, Amy S., 26
Whitaker, Todd, 90, 91
Williams, M. E., 54
Wolf, Dany, 26
Woods, R., 20

Yeager, David Scott, 54

Zimmerman, Jonathan, 63

About the Authors

Chad Prosser is the principal at Statesboro High School, a public high school in Georgia serving grades nine through twelve. He previously served as an administrator at a Georgia middle school, serving grades six through eight, and as a high school math teacher. During his time at Statesboro High School, Mr. Prosser contributed to revamping the processes of how school improvement plans and master schedules were created. He has been recognized as 2010–2011 Statesboro High School Teacher of the Year, Leadership Bulloch Class of 2011, 2017 Region 2-AAAAA Athletic Director of the Year, and one of *The Statesboro Herald*'s 2018 Top 20 Under 40.

Denise Spirou is the founding head of school at The Greene School, an independent pre-K through eighth grade school for high-performing students in West Palm Beach, Florida. Dr. Spirou created the curriculum and culture at Greene, nearly tripling enrollment in under three years. She joined the school after a sixteen-year tenure at another Florida private school for gifted children where she worked as a teacher and administrator, burnishing her credentials as one of the region's leading educators. Due to her extensive knowledge and experience, Dr. Spirou is in demand as an instructor for gifted coursework, workshops, and leadership training. Dr. Spirou's personalized connection with all her constituents makes her a powerhouse in academic leadership.

Jeffrey L. Buller is a senior partner in ATLAS: Academic Training, Leadership, and Assessment Services. He has served in administrative positions ranging from department chair to vice president for academic affairs at four very different institutions: Loras College, Georgia Southern University, Mary Baldwin College, and Florida Atlantic University. He is the author of nineteen other books on education leadership, a textbook for first-year college students, and a book of essays on the music dramas of Richard Wagner. Dr. Buller has also written numerous articles on Greek and Latin literature, nineteenth- and twentieth-century opera, and college administration. From 2003–2005, he served as the principal English-language lecturer at the International Wagner Festival in Bayreuth, Germany. More recently, he has been active as a consultant to the Ministry of Education in Saudi Arabia, where he is assisting with the creation of a kingdom-wide Academic Leadership Center. Along with Robert E. Cipriano, Dr. Buller works through ATLAS to provide leadership training and consultancy all over the world.